LOVE ATOP A KEYBOARD: A MEMOIR OF LATE-LIFE LOVE

Author: Janet Silver Ghent

Publisher: Mascot Books

ISBN: 978-1-63755-822-5

Rights: Worldwide

Format: Paperback Original

Pages: 288

Size: 6" x 9"

List Price: Paperback $18.95 US | $24.95 CAN

Genre:

BIO026000 BIOGRAPHY & AUTOBIOGRAPHY / Personal Memoirs

TRV001000 TRAVEL / Special Interest / Adventure

BIO037000 BIOGRAPHY & AUTOBIOGRAPHY / Jewish

For inquiries, please contact:

Janet Silver Ghent

ghentwriter@gmail.com

www.amplifypublishinggroup.com

Love Atop a Keyboard: A Memoir of Late-Life Love

For more information, please contact:
Mascot Books, an imprint of Amplify Publishing Group
620 Herndon Parkway, Suite 220
Herndon, VA 20170
info@mascotbooks.com

Library of Congress Control Number: 2023912291
CPSIA Code: PRV0723A
ISBN-13: 978-1-63755-822-5

Printed in the United States

For Allen

LOVE ATOP A KEYBOARD

A MEMOIR OF LATE-LIFE LOVE

JANET SILVER GHENT

PART I

SINGLE AGAIN

▌▌▌ ▌▌

CHAPTER 1

SPRING BREAK

April 1988

Spring break began in Los Angeles with a joyful Passover seder at the home of my daughter's college friend. Seven days later, it ended in San Diego with the prelude to a divorce.

That last evening, a Friday, my husband and I went to a symphony performance with our daughter, a student at San Diego State. When he and I returned to our motel room, I suddenly looked up at him and said, "This is our last vacation together."

Looking back, I will never know what possessed me to make that prescient pronouncement. However, the week's unspoken silences combined with memories of the previous summer in Scandinavia probably triggered my outburst. At home, with the distractions of work and family, my marriage was tolerable. On vacation, it was not.

In 1987, when we traveled to Scandinavia with our son and with my brother, my rising tension was palpable. While my husband and our son were resting in the hotel, my brother and I walked into Oslo's city center and sipped beer at an outdoor table. I think we both knew my marriage of twenty-two years was terminal, and we spoke of the unspeakable. Divorce, I told my brother, was inevitable.

"It's not a question of *what*," I said, "but *when*."

When was April 8, 1988, that eighth night of Passover. Responding to my pronouncement after the concert, my husband nodded, measuring his words carefully.

"Yes," he said. "Before we left for San Diego, I signed a one-month lease on a furnished apartment in San Francisco. It begins in two days. On Sunday, I'm moving out."

I clutched my stomach and took a deep breath. Then I nodded.

"A trial separation," he said, by way of explanation. Then he added that our week in San Diego had been pretrial. If it turned out well, he'd stay. If it didn't, well . . .

Momentary shock gave way to relief as I felt my tension dissipate. My husband was given to inscrutable silences, not anger, not words. I had no way of knowing he was on the threshold of leaving, nor did I know that I had been on trial. My vacation pronouncement was just what he needed to push him out the door.

This time I didn't beg him to stay. I had done my crying. For four or more years, intermittent waves of unspoken tension had become more frequent, more intense, even though we rarely fought. He had a girlfriend. He broke up with her. They got together again. They broke up. Each time, I tried to forgive, living in fear that he would leave, striving to maintain the status quo. After all, we had two teenagers. We owed it to them. In addition, I had no idea how I was going to survive on my salary as a reporter at a newspaper that was constantly in crisis. Where would I live? How would I pay the bills? Who would pay the college tuition?

Despite those concerns, that Friday night in San Diego I was determined to let him go, and my fears subsided as my uncertainty ended. This time the trial would be his, not mine. I removed my wedding ring and never wore it again. It was time to start over, as a single woman at the age of forty-five.

Maybe the seder was the final step, bringing home the joys of Judaism and my regrets about the course of my marriage. I realized what I had missed out on by not creating a Jewish home for my children, let alone for myself. But I didn't know how. My nonobservant, assimilated family hadn't provided me with the training. Moreover, my ex-Protestant atheist husband, who was vehemently anti-religion, had expressly forbidden such a step, so we had settled on what was called the demilitarized zone for interfaith marriages: Unitarianism. I was free to be Jewish, on my own, he said, but I couldn't bring it into the home or share the faith of my ancestors with my children: he called that "indoctrination." At the same time, my daughter was converting to evangelical Christianity—a great way to get saved and send Mother to Hell, I joked—and I was angry. Angry with her, angry with my husband, but most of all, angry with myself for dismissing my birthright.

Several weeks earlier, I had interviewed Elie Wiesel for the *Oakland Tribune*, where I was a features writer. When I let him know that "I happen to be Jewish," he looked me in the eye and said, "Don't happen to be Jewish. Be Jewish." The words of the eminent Holocaust writer, my increasing identification with my Judaism, and the experience of the Passover seder helped bring me back.

For many years, I had resisted Jewish observance for fear it would end my marriage. At the end of that week, my resistance ebbed. Even before my husband told me he was leaving, I was partly out the door, religiously speaking. Then when he said he wanted a trial separation, I did everything possible to not make him change his mind.

After checking out of our motel on Saturday, we stopped at my daughter's dorm to deliver the news in person. She had heard that pronouncement twice before, so it's hard to know whether she fully believed that this time was really the end. What I do know was that it helped to solidify her commitment to

Christianity, which offered her a refuge and a community during a difficult time.

Then we drove back to the Bay Area in silence. Uncharacteristically, I sped along Interstate 5 when I took the wheel. When we arrived home, I slept in my daughter's room. On Sunday morning, I left the house and busied myself with errands. When I returned, I ignored my husband as he packed and filled the car. As he was ready to leave, he stood at the front door and tried to deliver a rehearsed goodbye speech. I refused to listen. Nor would I look at him.

CHAPTER 2

EVERYBODY'S GETTING MARRIED BUT JANET

1964

When I returned to New York from Oberlin in June 1964, my family was proud of my cum laude degree. But now they were anxious for me to take the next step. It wasn't about career.

"Everybody's getting married but Janet!" my twelve-year-old brother taunted. "Karen's getting married in September, Linda's already married, Eleanor *was* engaged. Everybody but Janet."

My parents thought his teasing was cute. I did not. Marriage was not an immediate goal. I wanted to become a book editor, or a theater reviewer, or at the very least a journalist. Nevertheless, my family's gibes stung.

"How does marriage and children fit in with your plans?" my mother snickered, shaking her head.

"Janet thinks she can be a theater critic!" my father sneered. "There are only three or four people in the whole country that make a living at it. Dream on!"

Then he repeated the words of his longtime never-married assistant: "Tell Janet not to do what I did."

While we waited in line for the Frick Museum to open, my mother and I couldn't help eavesdropping on a couple of fiftyish singles in front of us.

"Listen to them," she said. "Sure, they travel, they enjoy outings, but their lives are so empty. Now it's too late for them. I don't want you to end up like them."

I just shook my head.

It didn't take me long to find a job, as a manuscript typist for *Holiday* magazine, making seventy-five dollars a week and spending a good portion of my salary on twenty-five dollars junior petite dresses from Bonwit Teller. Just before payday, with maybe a dollar or two in my wallet, I would walk along Fifth Avenue to the Central Park Zoo, the haunt of my early childhood. I would order a fruit bowl and an iced coffee at the cafeteria overlooking the seals and read a book. Despite my low salary—typical for young women seeking entry positions in publishing—I enjoyed the glamorous atmosphere at *Holiday*, the opportunity to attend screenings and write short query notes to the likes of Kingsley Amis and Cleveland Amory. I also was given the opportunity to copyedit, research, and write captions, at no additional pay. I hoped to be promoted to researcher, the intermediate step between typist and editor, but as I soon found out, *Holiday*'s parent company, Curtis Publishing, was in trouble and editors were quitting.

Meanwhile, friends and relatives fixed me up with marriageable Jewish men. I had a couple of dates with an obese rabbi from the Midwest who was new in town. On the plus side, he loved opera and theater, and he introduced me to the Second City troupe. On the minus side, he'd order two Napoleons for dessert and then put saccharine in his coffee. One night he phoned our home when I was still at work. My brother answered the phone.

"I was wondering if your sister would like to have dinner with me tonight," the rabbi said.

My brother, who knew I wasn't especially fond of the rabbi, replied: "I think she was planning on dining at home." That ended that.

Then Eleanor, no longer engaged, gave my phone number to an attorney whom she had dated once. He was too short for her. I was short with him. Later, Eleanor conned me into joining her at a Jewish singles dance in Scarsdale, where I met a Lactopine bath oil salesman. When I told him my grandmother adored Lactopine Swiss Pine Oil, he perked up, suggesting I try the new mimosa line. I never did. When the Lactopine salesman asked for my phone number, I changed a few digits. He dropped us off in Manhattan, and Eleanor and I took the subway and laughed all the way back to Queens.

I also dated Al Lubetnik (last name changed), a Princeton graduate student. When my little brother asked me whom I was going out with that evening, I told him Al Lubetnik. My brother began chorusing "Al Lubetnik, *gentil* Al Lubetnik" to the tune of "Alouette," and the nickname "Gentil" caught fire in the family. But by December, when Gentil didn't call to make plans for New Year's Eve, I phoned him at Princeton. Annoyed at my pushiness, he broke up with me.

Around that time, my great-aunt Stella introduced me to Larry, an NYU Law student. When Larry and I went to a French restaurant with two of his law school buddies and their nineteen-year-old brides, the women bragged about the upscale Manhattan venues where they had held their sweet-sixteen parties. I chimed in, apparently with a touch of disdain: "I had mine at home." Larry didn't ask me out for New Year's Eve.

I also had a single date with Adam, a third cousin. He told his mother, who told my mother, that I was too idealistic for his tastes.

Finally, there was Ben, a Cornell graduate student with whom I had hitchhiked in Europe during my junior year abroad. I almost became engaged to Ben, twice. The last time, I wore his Phi Beta Kappa key for a month or so. But Ben was verbally abusive, in a smug-history-professor kind of way. When he refused to look at my poetry, saying, "Shall we say, 'I love you in spite of your poetry'?" that sealed it for me. But he kept calling.

Ben reached me one night at Eleanor's house, where we were recording a demo of a song she had written, "I Want a Beatle for Christmas." Ben's reaction to our recording foray: "Oh, you're branching out!" I told Ben we were done. Meanwhile, the song also went nowhere.

With my social life in stagnation and *Holiday* magazine in trouble as four top editors suddenly resigned, I decided to take advantage of the fellowship Oberlin awarded me: all of $625, which paid for a semester's out-of-state tuition at University of Michigan.

Said one of the editors: "That's the best reason for leaving I've heard yet!"

I spent New Year's Eve in Greenwich Village with a girlfriend. The next day, I flew to Michigan to begin a master's program in English. I didn't know whether a master's would help in my career, but the University of Michigan had another advantage: the proximity of eligible, intelligent males whose relatives didn't know mine.

Just a few weeks after I arrived in Ann Arbor, I was sitting in the library reading a reserve book for my American intellectual history class and smoking a cigarette. (Yes, I used to smoke, which was permitted in some of the libraries.) Suddenly a note came sailing across the table: "Hi, would you like to go over to the Union for coffee?"

The sender, who was peering above a tome called *Unfair Trade Practices*, looked bored. However, he seemed harmless enough, so I said yes. After all, it was only coffee. Three weeks later, we were engaged. No, he wasn't Jewish. He called himself a WAS, omitting the P since he had left Protestantism behind in his freshman year. His parents, who were kind and unassuming in a Midwestern sort of way, had stopped attending church years ago. In contrast to my own excitable family, I found them calming and assuring. Maybe that was part of the appeal.

Did I have second thoughts? When my roommate Roberta asked me, "Do you want to marry this man, or do you just want to get married?" did I flinch? I don't remember. Soon the nuts and bolts of planning a wedding and purchasing a trousseau swept me away, pushing my qualms aside: I picked out patterns for flatware and china, ordered invitations and thank-you notes, and shopped for a wedding dress. Then I booked honeymoon motels on Cape Cod and Nantucket. Bye, bye, Janet. Soon I would be a Sadie.*

---

* "Sadie, Sadie" from *Funny Girl*, 1964.

CHAPTER 3

VIEW FROM THE MIDDLE OF THE BRIDGE

1965

*O*n August 1, in the back seat of my parent's car, I looked wistfully at the familiar landmarks: the United Nations buildings against the East River, the Empire State and Chrysler buildings towering on the horizon. But with my parents in the front seat, and my wedding dress and shoes in the trunk, this journey across the Queensboro Bridge marked a transition. There is no turning back in the middle of a bridge.

At age twenty-two, I was among the last of the girls from the old neighborhood to tie the knot. It wasn't just my friends from home. During my last year at Oberlin, I attended myriad bridal showers and several weddings. A few of those Oberlin women are still married to their first husbands. Such was not the case with Eleanor, Linda, or Karen, the girls from the old neighborhood.

Twenty-three years later, with one child in college and one in high school, I was one of the last of my childhood friends to divorce. The day my husband walked out, I bought jumper cables. That night I had to use them.

Yet I was the one who got the jump start. Until my ex walked out the door, I didn't realize how unhappy I had been. Now I was no longer a passenger. I was in the driver's seat, crossing new bridges.

CHAPTER 4

TRADING BETTER-THAN-NOTHING FOR OUTRIGHT UNCERTAINTY

1984-1988

*T*he first time my ex dropped the bomb, we were in New York, visiting my family. It was Christmastime 1984, and we had spent a glorious Christmas Eve at my parents' home in the Hamptons, where my mother had pasted colorful holiday bows on a potted ficus tree. Earlier that day, we had ambled along the Currier and Ives streets of Easthampton. We were with our children, my brother, and one of his friends, and I couldn't have been happier. On Christmas Day, we returned to the city, camping at my brother's apartment in Brooklyn Heights before planning a day in Manhattan. We had matinee tickets to Tom Stoppard's *The Real Thing,* starring Glenn Close and Jeremy Irons, and I was excited. I love Christmastime in the city, and I was half in love with Jeremy Irons.

On December 26, when we awoke, my husband wanted to make love. I wanted to get a head start on our day in the city and wasn't in the mood. Right then and there, he told me he wanted a divorce. He would be leaving after we returned home.

No, he didn't have a girlfriend, but he had one in mind, as I would soon find out. While the sexual revolution was playing, he had missed out. Then he arrived just as they were rolling the credits.

I ran into the shower and let the water rain over me. I couldn't look at him, and I didn't want to say much. Nonetheless, there we were, together in New York, on vacation. We had tickets to a show that neither of us wanted to miss. The rest of the day I walked in a haze. I ate nothing but bagels and blueberry muffins, washed down with bad tea. I don't remember the play. A couple of good-looking actors were on stage, reciting lines, just words.

After the play, we went to my parents' apartment in Forest Hills, where our children were staying. I walked into my parents' bedroom alone and told them what had transpired. My father paused, looked at my mother, and then looked at me.

"We're surprised it lasted as long as it did," he said.

It was no secret that my parents were not fond of my ex, but they had managed to keep it cordial. On our last night before leaving the city, my ex and I slept in my father's office, a pied-à-terre on Lower Madison Avenue, made love, and managed to reconcile. But a week or so later, when I was at work at the *Oakland Tribune*, I phoned his office and was told he had taken a vacation day. That was a surprise. When he arrived home, I asked him where he had been.

Stone-faced, he said, "I had a date."

A date? Who was she? Was it the massage instructor from our retreat at Asilomar, the zaftig poetry maven who propositioned him, or the inebriated woman who danced with a kazoo at her party in Berkeley?

It was the kazoo lady, and they had spent his vacation day in bed.

Once again, he was planning to leave me. Once again, I cried, begged, cajoled. Once again, we reconciled. He bought me what we called a "recommitment ring," with tiny emeralds and diamonds. We also went to Europe, and he pledged his love on the Pont Neuf in Paris.

But all was not well. One evening I had just returned home from an interview in Berkeley with author and environmentalist Frances Moore Lappé when he confronted me. He waited until the children were in bed.

"We need to talk," he said.

Uh-oh.

"Do you love me?" he asked.

I nodded.

"Good, because it's going to take a lot of love to get through this. I've been living a double life."

A double life? I thought he was going to tell me he was gay, but no. It turned out he had just asked the kazoo lady to marry him. She said no. She had another lover, a sexy chemist from the East Coast.

Once again, I persuaded him to stay. I didn't see how I could support two teenagers on a reporter's salary. I had an exciting career, first as a fashion editor at the *Contra Costa Times*, then as a features writer and an occasional columnist at the *Oakland Tribune*. (Both newspapers have since merged as the *East Bay Times*.) I was winning awards. I had wonderful colleagues who bucked me up when I was low. My marriage wasn't perfect, but I was content.

In Susan Page's book *If I'm So Wonderful, Why Am I Still Single?** she describes the better-than-nothing relationship. The BTN keeps many singles in less-than-wonderful relationships because they can count on dates for Saturday nights, New Year's Eves, and major holidays. Maybe my marriage itself was a BTN. For almost twenty-three years, what kept me in the marriage was mostly our children.

---

* I interviewed Susan Page in 1988, when the book was first published by Viking. Since then, the best-selling book has been reissued and translated into eighteen languages.

Like the women of my mother's generation, I was traditional, and I stuck it out. My ex knew I wasn't happy, even before I allowed myself to acknowledge it. After he finally walked out, he said, "Believe me, you left."

CHAPTER 5

COMING HOME TO JUDAISM

When I was growing up, being Jewish meant we couldn't have as big a Christmas tree as the Italian family who lived upstairs. It also meant that every few years, my parents would decide we couldn't have a Christmas tree at all, "because it wasn't right."

In our Jewish neighborhood in Rego Park, New York, our family was different. We never had a menorah and never celebrated Hanukkah, never went to synagogue, unless we were invited to somebody's bar mitzvah, never fasted on Yom Kippur. I was in the fourth generation of a mostly German-Jewish family. In the process of becoming Americanized, my ancestors had given up on organized religion. My parents used to say that they never denied they were Jewish. But they never affirmed it either. Being Jewish had more to do with concerns about anti-Semitism and the Holocaust, gentlemen's agreements, and avoiding Jewish expressions in the company of non-Jews. I used to joke that my parents never used Yiddish words until they heard them uttered by Johnny Carson.

Christmas, as we celebrated it, had more to do with Irving Berlin and Mel Tormé (both Jewish) than with Jesus. We had songfests and family skits, great food, and plenty of gifts. When Jewish friends told me it wasn't right to celebrate Christmas, I assumed it was because they were jealous. Rabbinical tracts on the topic of "Why Jews Shouldn't Celebrate Christmas" didn't impress me either. In fact, they drove me away, mostly because they contained a negative message, defining Jews in terms of what they aren't. Such messages make little impact on a person who has no positive concept of what it means to be Jewish.

In addition, some of these tracts were filled with what I thought were half-truths: the Christmas tree symbolizes the cross; the holly berries symbolize the blood of Jesus; the evergreen symbolizes eternal life through Jesus. I didn't buy any of these statements. In college, I learned that all these symbols came from pagan rituals that existed long before the birth of Jesus, who was probably not born on December 25. As a nonobservant Jew, I felt no qualms about celebrating what I viewed as a winter solstice festival rooted in pagan tradition. Later, when I married a non-Jewish atheist, I decided that my children would grow up with memories of magic that included Santa Claus. I handmade ornaments for our spectacular tree.

Some Jewish friends asked me how I could turn away from my Jewish heritage. The truth of the matter is that it was a legacy that was never passed on to me. And as I grew older, I developed a hunger for the spiritual nourishment I had lived without for so long. The Unitarian Universalist church I had joined, with its secular humanist approach, did not feed my soul. What I witnessed was a great deal of experimentation, trying on bits and pieces from a variety of religious traditions. I didn't want to wear a costume. I wanted my own clothes back. My Jewish clothes.

While I was working on a series about the Jewish Renewal movement, a rabbi recommended that I read Paul Cowan's book *An Orphan in History: Recovering a Jewish Legacy*. It opened my eyes. Here was a former Christmas-tree Jew who had found his own spiritual roots. I also had some helpful conversations with

Barbara Steinberg, a licensed clinical social worker with Jewish Family Service of the Greater East Bay. What helped is that my background did not shock her. She told me I didn't have to feel guilty about my attraction to Christmas.

"We are often attracted to things that are not our own," she said. "People don't feel deprived if what they hold to is rich."

In 1987, after much ambivalence, I bought my last Christmas tree. But the excitement and joy I had once felt were missing. I also lit Hanukkah candles. Something deep inside me began to glow. And it was a light that wouldn't go out. The following Passover, I was invited to a seder in Los Angeles. The spiritual light, kindled at Hanukkah, began to burn more brightly. The seder did for me what all of those "Why Jews Shouldn't Celebrate Christmas" tracts never had. It brought me to self-discovery, not through guilt but through joy and affirmation. I didn't need Christmas anymore.

CHAPTER 6

WHY AM I DOG-PADDLING IN A DUCK POND?

1988-1992

*M*y return to Judaism converged with becoming single at age forty-five. My writing also began to take on new directions, and my editor moved me from Styles to the Currents beat, which some of us quipped "nuts and sluts." I interviewed off-the-wall celebrities with books or products to promote, and I explored a wide range of topics: "Dancing for Klutzes," "Codependent or Confused?," "Menopause: The Pause that Distresses."

In 1988, just after the split with my first husband, I wrote a feature on astrology, meeting up with Joan Quigley, Nancy Reagan's astrologer. By way of preparation, Quigley had requested that I send the date, time, and city of my birth so she could prepare a set of cassette tapes pinpointing not only my sign—Scorpio on the cusp of Libra—but also how the sun, moon, and all the planets fit into the mix.

"You have a very sexy sign!" she told me. "You won't be single for long."

Astrologically speaking, twelve years may not be a long time. However, I passed through many lives in what I call my interregnum, the interval between marriages, and I often felt I was suspended above an abyss without a safety net. Quigley, who chose never to marry, didn't provide me with any pointers. However, I encountered several mavens who made a living offering advice:

- Go where the ducks are. If you're a woman seeking a man, don't expect to find him in the library stacks or a book group. Join a hiking group, ski, head to the gym.
- Master the art of mingling.
- Don't count on friends for introductions. That worked in college, or in your twenties, when the pool of eligible singles was large. In your forties and fifties, that pool is a puddle.
- Personals ads: Not a bad way to expand your database, but always meet in a public place and keep the meeting short, opting for coffee, not dinner.
- You may have to kiss a few frogs before you find a prince, but if the frog is slimy, don't kiss him. An acquaintance of mine thought she'd landed a prince. He was gorgeous, he was affluent, he was an alcoholic, and he was gay.
- Don't settle for a better-than-nothing relationship.
- Don't give up.

When I first became single, the ducks in the East Bay converged Sunday nights at the Lafayette Orinda Presbyterian Church, where singles of all faiths gathered in the social hall for Shipmates events. At the time, Shipmates was a group of fortyish singles, although older men sauntered in to check out the younger women. In addition to the Sunday night gatherings, which included lectures and discussion groups, Shipmates offered a rich array of activities: hikes, outings, dances, sing-alongs, and dinners. The first time I went to the Sunday night meet-up, I was there as a reporter, writing on the local singles scene while I was still married. As a reporter, I found it easy to mingle and ask questions. However, as a newly single woman, I couldn't hide behind my reporter's notebook. When I tried to slip inconspicuously into the big room for the meet and greet, a woman who knew me as married did a double take.

"YOU?" she said.

Had I fallen into a rabbit hole? Was I splashing in a putrid duck pond? Was I still me?

A lecture followed the meet and greet. Speakers would address such topics as where and how to find your mate or date. After that came the Afterglow, i.e., more meet, greet, and exchange of phone numbers.

That first evening as a single, I sat next to an Israeli-born professor I'll call Josh the Jerk and his friend Vince the Victim. They introduced me to women who became friends as well as to the Bay Area Jewish Singles Hiking Club. Vince also introduced me to Charlie Cholesterol, with whom I had much in common—we were both writer-editors from New York—but his nutrition lectures over dinner became tiresome. Who wants to go out to dinner with a man who looks askance if you butter your bread?

Amid all these encounters, my ex kept phoning day and night.

"I'm ready to come home now," he said.

"We'll talk in the morning," I replied.

Did I waver? Sometimes, but when I thought it over, I couldn't reopen the wound.

Getting back to Josh, I found him intriguing, and we enjoyed hiking as well as attending symphony concerts. But something about him wasn't quite right. One afternoon when I was at his Oakland apartment, he received a call from a woman who was waiting for him outside a movie theater in San Francisco. He had apparently stood her up. I shrugged. Was this the lay of the land in the singles world?

Then something caught me completely off guard. Perusing the singles postings in the *Bay Guardian*, I came across an ad that sounded suspicious.

Something like fiftyish professor, physically fit, loves opera, symphony, hiking, seeks a like-minded slim, attractive thirtyish woman "with lots of body hair."

In the files at the *Oakland Tribune*, I found a picture of a bearded lady and sent a photocopy to Josh's post box at the *Guardian*. He knew it was from me. He was not amused. I should have known better, but Josh managed to hurt me, telling me off, letting me know that my jokes weren't funny. After I was a panelist on *The Oprah Winfrey Show*, for a discussion on "The Fashion Conspiracy," we watched the video together on a Saturday afternoon. He told me, "You were the most uptight person on the panel." Yet that same day, he took me to a faculty holiday dinner, bragging that I was a famous reporter. These days, I'm told, Josh is living in a retirement community with a trans man. For his sake, I hope his partner has lots of body hair.

Although I was an equal-opportunity dater, I really wanted to meet Jewish men, so I joined the Bay Area Jewish Singles Hiking Club. That's where I met Phyllis, who became my friend and my stockbroker, as well as a couple of guys with whom I had relationships of various lengths. I also attended Friday night services. One San Francisco synagogue held monthly post-service singles soirées in the social hall. That's where I met Eric (name changed). He was tall. He was thin. He had nice hazel eyes. He was a doctor. And he looked as if he were a few years older than I was, but not *too* old.

Hmmm, I thought. *A possibility.*

So often at these singles affairs, I would wind up talking to men in their thirties, who were driven crazy by women in their thirties, who were driven crazy by the ticking of their biological clocks. They would seek me out for refuge.

Eric, however, was older. I sashayed over.

"Hi, I'm Janet."

"Hi," he said. "I saw you talking to Peter. How do you know Peter?"

"Through my hiking club," I said.

"You've got good legs. Are you a biker too?" he said, his hazel eyes lighting up.

I blushed. Then I countered with a risky gambit. "I guess they're not bad for middle-aged legs."

His hazel eyes clouded over.

"You're middle-aged?" he said, letting me know that he was fifty-two and had a two-year-old son from a very brief marriage.

"Tell me," he said. "Are there any attractive women in your hiking club who are about twenty-eight? I want to get married again and have more children, but I don't want to get involved with a woman who is thirty-five-ish. I mean, amniocentesis is risky, and I don't want to have to go through all that. I'd rather find a younger woman."

Ouch.

"You know," I responded. "I really don't think my daughter would be interested in dating a man who is several years older than her father. Why don't you play with the kids your own age?"

"I already do," he said with a laugh. "My two-year-old. We're on the same level."

On that point, we agreed. I made my exit, got into my car, and drove across the bridge to the suburbs, trying to make sense of it all.

You blew it! I said to myself. *Don't you know that Rule No. 1 is to be cagey about your age? Didn't a male singles expert tell you never, ever, ever let a man know you are forty-something and have grown children?*

Only after the man has sworn his undying love, purchased honeymoon cruise tickets, and made a down payment on the house you'll share in the hills, only then can you tell him the truth. That you spent your grade-school years watching Howdy Doody *and the Army-McCarthy hearings. That you can sing the jingles for Ajax, Colgate toothpaste, Chevrolet, and Brylcreem. That you know where the yellow went. That you borrowed your teenager's Retin-A for your forehead lines but had to graciously relinquish it when he needed it for zits.*

I found myself wallowing in a big fat tub of middle-aged angst. Then I remembered Albert Ellis. No, I didn't meet him at a singles affair. He was a psychologist who launched Rational Emotive Behavior Therapy. One of Ellis's techniques was to talk back to your self-doubts, countering with the facts. Sometimes it worked.

You should be rejoicing, not crying, I said in my best nasal Albert Ellis voice. *Eric is a jerk, not you. By hinting at your age, you were able to waltz away in less than five minutes and not waste your time on a man who lacks character and isn't right for you.*

I smiled the rest of the way home. In 1989, Barbara Gordon was promoting her new book, *Jennifer Fever.* "Jennifer" was the generic name she gave to young women whom older men hankered after. And what was the moniker she used for the middle-aged woman who is dumped for younger women? She named her "Janet."

Well, this Janet was determined to strike back. I called in an expert: Judith Martin, better known as Miss Manners, who was in San Francisco promoting her new book.

The problem, said Martin, was that by choosing to put myself forward at a singles event, I was letting myself in for a potentially abusive, abrasive time.

At a more conventional social event, she said, the conversational pathway is smoother. There are meat and vegetables, so to speak. Gravy. Plenty of pleasant chitchat. An unwillingness to pick at raw nerves before the hors d'oeuvres have been cleared.

At many events geared specifically for singles, she said, there are no such buffers.

"That's the kind of thing you run into when you strip away the grace notes of society," she said. "You've gotten rid of the vegetables. That's why people complain that it's a meat market."

Yes, I thought to myself, remembering my encounter with Patrick, a man I met at a Sierra Singles dance. When I told him I was a journalist, he replied, "You know why there's no money in journalism? Because there are too many women in it."

I had two words for him. They weren't "Happy birthday."

During my twelve-year interregnum, I continued to attend singles events: discussion groups, hikes, religious services, and sing-alongs. I placed personals ads and joined a couple of choirs. I also continued to gape at the monkeys in the singles zoo, sometimes seeing myself. And I continued to gather material.

CHAPTER 7

CUTE DJF, NEWLY SINGLE, SEEKS WHAT?

1988–

*I*n addition to attending singles mixers and hiking with the Sierra Singles and the Bay Area Jewish Singles Hiking Club, I widened my database, posting and answering singles ads. In the pre-internet era, responses arrived by snail mail, relayed through a postbox. I received several letters from men who enclosed bare-chested photos.

Then there was a note from a "nice Jewish boy" who happened to live in the same apartment complex as my ex. We talked by phone. Then he called me again to invite me to a High Holiday dinner at his home. In the world of singles, that's a no-no. The rule is *always* meet in a public place.

As we continued the conversation, it became apparent to me that he was considerably more traditional than I was. When I let him know that I had been a Unitarian, had previously "married out," and had a daughter who was a born-again Christian, he turned hostile.

I let him know we were done.

He agreed. "When you're ready to become a real Jew, call me."

What I should have responded was, "And when you're ready to become a real mensch, I'll think about it." But I just hung up.

I had another experience with a man whose approach to Judaism didn't match mine. Ironically, he was the only person with whom I had been introduced by a mutual friend. He was a surgeon—every Jewish mother's dream. We went out a few times but drifted apart. We were Jewishly incompatible.

His pronouncements over dinner at an Italian restaurant let me know this wasn't going to work: "If my son were arrested, he would still be my son," he said. "If he told me he was gay, I would be upset, but I would come around. But if he married out, that would be the end."

I looked him in the eye and said, "A parent who cuts off a child in that way cuts himself off from God."

He shuddered.

"Do you really believe that, Janet?"

"Yes," I said. "I absolutely do."

Looking back, maybe I should have walked out then and there, but out of respect to our mutual friend and the tasty fettuccini in front of me, I finished dinner and let him pay.

Pursuing a Jewish surgeon might have made my parents happy. But this was my life. Determined not to let a couple of bad episodes end my pursuit, I continued to place ads and answer others. I met punsters, professors, accountants, teachers, and computer wizards. These encounters rarely led to a second date—except with a man I'll call David the Dating Amnesiac.

I had two first dates with David, who had a private plane and conducted business up and down the West Coast. I don't remember much about the *first* first date, except that I found him fit, charming, and good-looking. He said he would call me when he was next in the Bay Area.

I opened my calendar and told him I was booked for the next three weekends.

If he wanted to get together, we needed to set a date ahead of time.

He squirmed, saying he needed to be more spontaneous because he usually didn't know ahead of time when he would be in San Francisco. Anyway, the next time he called, I was busy. Since I was a new commodity on the singles scene, I was more popular than I had ever been in high school. That picture changed when I passed fifty. Then men my own age—or even ten years older— were seeking women in their thirties, putting me out of circulation. But back to David.

Several years after that first date, when I was working for what was then the *Jewish Bulletin,* I placed another ad in the newspaper. Once again, David responded. We had an informal lunch in San Francisco's Galleria shopping complex. I swear the entire time he was looking at his reflection in my glasses. Anyway, he had no recollection of ever having met me before and found it amusing that I remembered.

When I returned to the office, I relayed the experience.

"Oh, you're talking about David!" said Lisa (not her real name), a cute reporter in her early thirties. "I went out with him once, but he was much too old for me."

Then I mentioned the experience to Helene, my physical therapist, and Phyllis, my friend and financial adviser. Helene had gone out with him once and Phyllis was supposed to go out with him, but he stood her up. The next week at my women's group, I relayed the incident again.

"Oh, you mean David, the man with the airplane?" said Marilyn, a therapist who headed the group. "I actually went out with him twice. The second time, I invited him to a function where I needed an escort. He's very suave, I'll say that about him, which is why I invited him. Anyway, that was the beginning and the end."

Some months later, the *Jewish Bulletin* was hosting a singles gathering at the Citicorp building in San Francisco, and I attended along with coworkers. Bored after about forty-five minutes, I was on my way out when I passed a cadre of men congregating around the bar. There was David, looking as suave as ever. He called out to me.

"How can you leave before we've met?" he said.

"We've met," I replied. "I'm looking for someone who's interested in a real relationship, not someone who is trying to see how many women he can date once."

In my fantasy movie, Lisa, Helene, Phyllis, Marilyn, and I would surround David at a singles soirée and give him a piece of our collective minds, embarrassing the hell out of him. But like Narcissus, who falls in love with his own reflection, David would neither see nor hear us.

CHAPTER 8

BAD OCTOBERS

1989–1992

*O*nce again, it was October, which had been my favorite time of the year. October is the month of my birthday, a time of crisp air, brilliant leaves, hikes in the woods, new clothes, promises of new beginnings in both the Jewish calendar and the school year. In ninth grade, we had memorized Bliss Carman's "A Vagabond Song," a poem that spoke to me:

There is something in October sets the gypsy blood astir;
We must rise and follow her.

But as a single journalist in a moribund industry, working in a city in crisis, my Octobers were turning bleak.

The Loma Prieta earthquake hit at 5:04 p.m. on October 17, 1989. Just as I finished the final sentences of a first-person piece on rock climbing—a feat I undertook on a dare from my son—the ground shook underneath me. Over the years at the *Oakland Tribune*, we had become inured to the periodic rattling of the old-fashioned printing presses. But this time, an editor cried out, "It's not the presses!"

I grabbed my purse and ran to what I thought was a safer part of the Tribune Tower. Fissures pocked the floor. Then we evacuated the building, running down a shaky staircase with broken steps to the parking lot, where a condemned building had collapsed on three cars.

I phoned my son to tell him I was all right and asked him to post a note on the front door to cancel a scheduled meeting of a singles group; I would not be home on time. That evening, I drove to a hospital emergency room to speak with the injured and to a sports bar to get quotes. The earthquake had damaged the Tribune Tower, destroyed the upper deck of the Bay Bridge, and halted the third game of the A's-Giants World Series before the first pitch was tossed at Candlestick Park. With the Bay Bridge closed, reporters returned to the newsroom via the San Mateo Bridge. One of them shouted, "Hey, A's in two." Happily, when the series resumed, the A's won after just four games.

My father, who was in a New York hospital for minor surgery, found out about the quake while waiting for the third game to begin. He was less alarmed than my mother, who phoned from Queens the next morning.

"You're *not* going to work today!" she pronounced.

"Mom, I'm a reporter, remember? This is what we do."

While my suburban home was untouched, the impact of the quake reverberated inside me, particularly during aftershocks. Alone and distraught on a Saturday night while my son was with his father, I threw myself into my work. With the Bay Bridge closed, I drove to a BART station to talk to suburbanites who had never used public transportation, and I managed to write a light reaction piece about their struggles with turnstiles and change machines.

We weathered that October crisis, but two years later, another followed. In October 1991, Oakland was in flames. The 1,520-acre Oakland East Bay Hills fire killed twenty-five people, injured 150 others, and destroyed more than three thousand houses and apartments.

Accompanied by a photographer, I visited the scarred hillsides where chimneys stood like tombstones. Crumbling homes were surrounded by tangled electrical wiring that seared my feet. Homeowners returned, calling out the names of pets.

"There's my living room," one man whispered as he peered at nothingness. Amid the destruction, a woman mourned her missing recipe collection, gleaned from her mother and grandmother. One homeowner turned philosophic, grateful that he and his family were able to get out: "I asked myself what was important. What did I need to save," he told me, "and the only thing I needed to save was my ass."

Later I visited a hospital burn unit and spoke with patients who had run down the hillside, abandoning their cars. They were the lucky ones. They survived. I asked one of the physicians why there were so few serious injuries. He said that in a fire of that magnitude, people either got out in a hurry, injury-free, or the fire consumed them. There was not much in between.

Not long after, the *Tribune* brought in a crisis counselor to speak to the reporters, but only a few of us showed up. Then, as always, work was our therapy.

I was used to writing about other people's crises, but in October 1992, when I turned fifty, the crisis was mine. That's what I told the national TV reporters who descended on the *Tribune* the day it was sold.

Like my marriage, the *Oakland Tribune* had almost died several times before it finally bit the dust. The Gannett newspaper chain, which bought the *Tribune* shortly before I was hired in 1980, dumped the paper three years later, "selling" it to editor and publisher Robert Maynard by providing a substantial loan. Over the next decade, the independent newspaper was rescued more than once and even won a Pulitzer Prize for photographic coverage during the 1989 earthquake. Then in 1991, we earned kudos for our coverage of the Oakland East Bay Hills firestorm. Despite these awards, the newspaper had been hemorrhaging for years, with reductions in staff, reductions in pay and work hours, and repeated rumors of closing.

In October 1992, it was no longer a rumor. Maynard, who was fighting prostate cancer (he died the following August), had kept the newspaper open with loans from Gannett. But that October, just as I sold my suburban home and was in escrow on a townhouse nearer to work, he sold the *Tribune* to the Alameda Newspaper Group. Suddenly I was jobless.

My dream condominium in Alameda was waiting in escrow, but without a job, I couldn't qualify for a mortgage, so the townhouse sale was kaput.

"I thought it was a done deal," my real estate agent said.

Fifty, single, homeless, and jobless.

In the meantime, awaiting what had turned out to be the foiled closure of the townhouse, I had been camping in a friend's San Francisco apartment. What was next? Further complicating my life, I had two children in college, my ex-husband had lost his job of twenty-six years when his company was sold, and my small alimony payments had ceased. Then my daughter announced her engagement, and I had a wedding to plan, along with the expenses.

When friends asked me where I was going, I joked that I was moving to Cleveland. That wasn't out of the question. Indeed, representatives from newspapers throughout the country were interviewing *Tribune* reporters. But they were primarily seeking young minority writers and editors to diversify their newsrooms. After a series of interviews with editors from Los Angeles, New York, the Bay Area, and yes, Cleveland, I was still out of a job the day the *Tribune* closed, surviving on severance pay, unemployment, and money from the sale of my house.

Concerned about finances, I took the first job I was offered, as a publication editor at a state university. The pay was good, but I was miserable. Like the patrons at *Cheers*, I was used to being in a place where I knew people, where they knew my name, where I had a byline. At fifty, I was fifty miles from anywhere I called home, with no community, no friends nearby, and nobody who knew my name.

My living situation compounded my anxiety. What I thought was an attractive air-conditioned apartment, with a private terrace and a rooftop pool, had liabilities. If I took a shower, it set off the smoke alarm. I soon discovered that my luxury apartment overlooked an all-night-drive-through Jack in the Box. On Thursday and Sunday nights, which happened to be date nights in town, I would awaken at 2:00 a.m. to the sounds of honking and car radios blasting rap: "*Boom chicka, boom chicka.*"

I complained to the landlord. I complained to the Jack in the Box owner. I complained to the police department. Nothing happened.

Within a week of accepting the job, I knew I had made a mistake. My colleagues treated me as if I were a Martian. They told me I "didn't understand the corporate culture," that I seemed to view the institution with a reporter's perspective, like an outsider. I hadn't "bought in."

Corporate culture? It was a bureaucracy.

Then I was asked to do a question-and-answer interview with the acting university president. My supervisor sat in on the interview, but she and her supervisor didn't like what the president had to say, so they rewrote his statements and recrafted my story. But they conceded that the piece was no longer a *Q and A*. After all, lying they knew was a sin.

In the midst of all this, plus traveling back and forth to San Diego to plan my daughter's wedding, I had a breast-cancer scare. Fortunately, it was just an inflamed lymph node. One of my colleagues suggested I meet with the university's in-house therapist. At her suggestion, I visited a psychologist.

"Clinical depression," he pronounced, adding that my colleagues were looking for an excuse to fire me.

I knew it. So did my parents, who just shook their heads when they visited.

One summer evening I took a walk through a rose garden where I felt at one with the blighted blooms. With yellow legal pad in hand, I wrote about "the garden of withered roses, where I move among the ashes. . . . I am writing and I am crying, sobbing."

A day or so later, I was called into my supervisor's office. She had prepared her speech, with help from the HR department.

"As you know, things aren't going well," she said. "I have a letter. You don't need to read it now."

Bottom line: I was not being recommended for permanent employment. I would be paid for another two weeks, but that day in July 1993 was my last day at my desk. My supervisor handed me a checklist: return keys, visit HR, return books to the library. If I wished, I could make an appointment with the university counselor for one last free visit, but I didn't want to. Strangely enough, the so-called clinical depression I had been experiencing suddenly lifted.

By the next October, my bleak aura was dissipating. I had moved to Oakland, to an apartment with a great view of the hills and a distant view of Lake Merritt. I freelanced for private clients. Then I read that the *Jewish Bulletin*, forerunner to *J. The Jewish News of Northern California*, was seeking a copy editor. Along with my resume, I enclosed a chutzpadik letter: "Why am I applying for a job at the *Jewish Bulletin* when I know you pay *bupkes* (Yiddish for *diddly-squat*)?"

I was hired.

My embarrassingly low salary required belt-tightening, but with the help of freelancing and a substantial down payment from the sale of my suburban home, I was able to purchase a townhouse in Alameda a few doors down from the one I had lost. I found solace on my small enclosed patio, growing herbs and roses. My flowers thrived.

I joined a synagogue that was walking distance from my townhouse, made friends, walked along the canals and the bay, and I began to study the Torah. This was my new life.

I still grappled with loss. Every time I drove past the Tribune Tower on the freeway, I cried. Yet I remembered the words of Sylvia Boorstein, who married the teachings of Buddhism and Judaism in several books. Buddhism teaches that nothing is permanent. Expecting permanence, we suffer.

This too shall pass, I would say to myself as I nodded off to sleep. Those words, my new community, and the teachings and rituals of my own faith helped me pull through. My Octobers were getting better.

CHAPTER 9

*WITH METHOD IN MY MADNESS, I REVISIT THE PERSONALS**

1995

I began 1995 with several New Year's resolutions. The first was to end an on-again, off-again four-year relationship. We cared for one another deeply, but we couldn't live together, and both of us knew it.

Next, I tried to get rid of my stray grays. Whatever I tried didn't work for long. Twenty-five years later, amid the coronavirus, I learned to love that gray, but in my early fifties, I wasn't ready. After touching up my hair as best I could, I bought a couple of cute outfits in the "weekend wear" category for brunches and cappuccino klatches.

---

* An earlier version of this chapter appeared February 24, 1995, in the *Jewish Bulletin of Northern California*.

My final step was the *Jewish Bulletin*'s Such-a-Match page—the personal ads that ran in newsprint. I was going to take the plunge, again. One advantage of working for the newspaper was that I didn't have to pay to play. Plus, I could see the responses as they came in.

At the time, I was searching for a partner, but as a "method" reporter and editor, I also had my eyes on an article. One way to maintain my sanity in the meshugge (crazy) world of singles was to turn a love quest into an experiment and a story.

My goal was to find out what kind of singles ad would really work and whether I would find my *beshert*—my meant-to-be partner—if I skipped the Mozart, candlelight, and sunset walks along the beach, and instead wrote a brutally honest blurb. But I didn't write just one ad. I wrote three.

The first was in hyperbolic, stereotypical personals-ad style. Note standard abbreviations: DJF is divorced Jewish female, N/S is nonsmoking, N/D is nondrinking.

Pretty, Witty, Bright

Slim, petite, active brunette who enjoys repartee seeks match. You have big heart, flat tummy, talent with words and appetite for life and love. N/S, N/D, 45-55.

Then I tried something more offbeat:

New Homeowner Seeks Handyman

Cute, petite DJF who's great in the kitchen seeks mensch 45-57 who's terrific in the rest of the house. You're kind, bright, fit, career-minded and tired of being alone—and you love theater, good music and the outdoors. N/S, N/D.

Finally, I wrote my no-nonsense, cut-to-the chase ad revealing my age and the fact that I was seeking the big "C": commitment. Yes, I know it's *chutzpa-dik* (audacious) for a woman of over fifty to request a partner who was below nursing-home age. But if you don't ask, you don't get:

It's Our Turn

Our careers are in full swing, our kids have flown. And we're ready to take a chance on the next phase. I'm an energetic extrovert, thin, short, 52, look 10 years younger, and have a great sense of humor. Love to sing, dance, read, hike, cook. You're a sweet, even-tempered guy, under 60, fit, who wants to share life with the right woman. N/S, N/D.

Within three weeks of publication, "It's Our Turn" received only two responses: one by voicemail, one by note. Both were in the (408) area code, centered around San Jose, making us geographically incompatible, as I lived in the East Bay and was a (510). (Ironically, the man I married was also in the "wrong" area code: He was a (650), as in the northern end of the South Bay. But by that time, I was older and less picky.)

One of the responders answered all three ads with Post-it notes, all ending: "If you live in the South Bay, let's meet for coffee and see if there's any compatibility and chemistry."

"Pretty, Witty, Bright" fared slightly better. One letter was memorable.

"Pretty, Witty, Bright" was scrawled in blue, after "Dear," on a photocopy of a handwritten note loaded with misspellings.

What is this? I said to myself. *Copy editor hell?*

I sat down at my computer and dashed off a response, which I did not mail:

Dear Mr. Badspeller:
"Pretty, Witty, Bright" received your form letter letting her know that you're "just too busy to write many persons individual letters."

Well, she is a copy editor who ekes out a living catching the kind of mistakes you letter is full of—like not capitalizing "french" and "spanish."

"Pretty, Witty, Bright" loves flattery. Particularly about her writing. But when you said, "Anyway, I really liked what you had to say in your add" (sic), she was less than convinced.

Much to my surprise, "New Homeowner Seeks Handyman" turned out to be the sleeper—and it didn't just attract handymen who told me they were great in the bedroom. Responses came from engineers, computer people, a lawyer, a Russian, an Israeli, and an electrician. It drew three guys who had gone to Brooklyn College.

And I had to move all this way from Queens to date a guy from Brooklyn? Go figure. I even heard from David the Date Amnesiac, who had answered my personals ad six years before. He had no recollection.

Meanwhile, back at the office, Jennie, the *Bulletin* bubbie (honorary grandma) and volunteer who sorted through the Such-a-Match responses, was following my odyssey through Singledom with interest. She brought me my stash of letters.

"He wrote to you last week!" she said, holding up the small white envelope from Mr. Post-it.

"This one looks nicer," she said, handing me a thin speckled envelope. "You're the only one he wrote to."

I opened the letter. It was well-written, in blue ink. He said, "Yes, I believe in marriage and family as a route to happiness in life." He was handy. He was Jewish. And he was not in the (408) area code.

I let Jennie read it.

"I like this one," she said. "Good, strong handwriting, and he knows how to write a letter. I think you should go out with him. Find out if he has a father."

Well, I met the letter writer, who was a mensch. We enjoyed a lovely walk along San Francisco Bay. Sadly, he never called again. Despite my disappointment, I didn't give up. In fact, I planned my next personals ad:

Pretty Old and Wise

Skip the cappuccino and hyperbole. Writer/editor, brunette with color-resistant grays, seeks self-accepting mensch. You're 45-55, you've been married, you've passed through the midlife crisis intact, and you're willing to play with a woman your own age. Please reply with a personal letter that will be screened for grammar, spelling, and sincerity.

CHAPTER 10

'IN DREAR NIGHTED DECEMBER'

The feel of not to feel it,
When there is none to heal it.
—JOHN KEATS

1997–1998

On Christmas Eve 1997, my year of bleak began. I was alone. I had ended my on-again, off-again relationship with a San Francisco photographer. Rex the Remote, a pathologically private professor whom I had been dating, was in a nearby state, surrounded by his family. But my own family was miles away. My son was in France, my daughter was spending Christmas with my ex, and my parents and brother were visiting cousins in New Hampshire.

Even though I had returned to Judaism and no longer celebrated Christmas, the holiday had always been a family time for me. When I was growing up, the extended family gathered at our house, and my brother and I put on a show, singing satirical songs about family members, political events, or whatever struck us at the time. Years later as a young mother, we sang carols, baked

Christmas cookies, and created homemade ornaments. I set aside most of those traditions and gave the ornaments to my daughter when I re-embraced Judaism.

Nonetheless, I missed the warmth and family togetherness that revolved around the December holidays, and Hanukkah is by no means the Jewish equivalent of Christmas. With nowhere to go on Christmas Eve, I sat on my sofa feeling sorry for myself as I listened to Rachmaninoff and Tchaikovsky. But the next day, I was determined to get out of the house, so I called my friend Mary, and we joined a Jewish singles group for a walk along the Alameda shore. Over lunch in a taqueria, I struck up a conversation with a man who had shared some of my experiences. He was a Jewish Unitarian; I was a lapsed Unitarian. He had been to the Unitarian summer conference at Asilomar; so had I, although in different years. We began talking about some of the people we both knew.

"Did you know Winston [not his real name]?" he said.

I told him that my friend Phyllis had been to Winston's wedding.

He looked at me quizzically. "Phyllis who?" he said.

I mentioned her last name. "Do you know her?"

"Yes," he said. "She's my ex."

The day after Christmas, I phoned Rex the Remote, who shared his delightful holiday anecdotes. I had nothing to contribute to the conversation, except my determination to put his feet to the fire. I knew the relationship couldn't continue in its present state. The distance wasn't just physical; it was emotional. During our year of dating, we had spent time together in towns halfway between our cities, enjoyed an amorous week on the Mendocino coast, and shared weekends when professional meetings brought him to San Francisco. In between, we emailed every night, sending newsy missives, but neither of us signed our emails "Love." We ended with a noncommittal "Take care." Meanwhile, he never invited me to visit his home, and the teenage daughter who lived with him was unaware of my existence. My parents wondered whether Rex was secretly married. I didn't think that was the case. Nonetheless, it became blatantly apparent to me that I was wasting my time.

With that in mind, I orchestrated a preemptive breakup. "If we're going to have a relationship, we need to see each other more often," I said on the phone. "I need to be able to visit you on your turf. I need to meet your family. If not, then I need to date other people and move on."

He hesitated. Then he told me the words no woman wants to hear. "There's no nice way to say this, Janet. I've enjoyed our time together, and I wish you all the best, but I'm not in love with you."

At the next meeting of my women's group, I couldn't stop the tears. My friends expressed their sympathy. My parents, however, delivered an I-told-you-so script that only made me feel worse.

"We knew all along that this was going nowhere!" they said. "You shouldn't have let this go on this long." Meanwhile, Karen, my lifelong best friend, offered words of advice: "You need to find a man who is crazy about you."

Sure, I thought to myself, *but where*? Synagogue? Forget about it! Eligible single men weren't there. The hiking club? The oldest men were too young, or if they weren't, they thought I was too old.

Some months later, I sent Rex an email, telling him that I had tried to get over him, unsuccessfully. When I returned home from work, I read his long reply. He began his email with the easy stuff. He had purchased a new car. While on a visit to California, he had experienced a gall bladder attack and had surgery. Then came the zinger: He was "head over heels in love" with a woman he had known professionally for some time. To add to the pain, I think her name was Janet, but I may be projecting. I stood in my kitchen, still with my coat on, unable to make dinner, unable to do anything. Then I called Mary.

"Meet me at the synagogue," she said. "There's a lecture on Kabbalah (Judaism's mystical tradition). You'll find it interesting. And do try to eat something."

I made myself a peanut butter sandwich and went to the lecture, delivered by a guest rabbi. He had diagrams of the sefirot, which are like chakras, or paths to the infinite and higher consciousness. I zoned out. Whenever someone tries to explain Kabbalah to me, showing me pictures and diagrams, I escape into my own sphere of consciousness. It's not that I flunked enlightenment. Buddhism and meditation, I get. I just don't do diagrams well. They remind me of aptitude tests. The ones that netted me a lower IQ.

I spent the next week crying. Even the death of a distant friend's father, someone I had never met, set me off. I knew the symptoms. I'd been here before. Depression, or what Holly Golightly in *Breakfast at Tiffany's* called the "mean reds." But then I remembered a Buddhist principle: nothing is forever. Not even pain. This too shall pass.

CHAPTER 11

TALKING TO THE WALL

1998

*I*n March 1998, at dusk on my first visit to Israel, I stood before the Western Wall in tears and pressed a paper between the cracks. "Please, God, find me a match." Following the breakup with Rex the Remote, I experienced a dark period. While I didn't expect a miracle, I would have welcomed one.

I'd had enough of the proverbial singles lifestyle, which had appealed to me ten years earlier, when I first became a party of one. I was weary of coffee dates, personals ads, dances, and mixers. I wanted out.

Taking a break from all that, I was in Jerusalem with other Jewish journalists, on a trip sponsored by Hadassah. In addition to touring Hadassah's hospitals and educational institutions, we had the opportunity to learn about the status of women in Israel. What we learned was that our female coreligionists in Israel don't have the same rights to worship freely as we Americans do. On Shabbat, I returned to the women's side of the Western Wall to pray with Women of the

Wall. The group, which includes women from all streams of Judaism, Reform to Orthodox, sought the right to worship at the Wall wearing prayer shawls and carrying Torahs. But Israel's religious authorities were denying them that privilege.

As we huddled in prayer, the Israeli women hushed us, ensuring that we muffle our voices so the belligerent men on the other side of the divider wouldn't throw stones at us. Meanwhile on the other side, men welcomed Shabbat boisterously, dancing the hora and singing spiritedly, which we were forbidden to do. I might as well have been a frightened Black teen at Little Rock Central in 1957, attempting to integrate a Southern high school. But this time, it wasn't the Orval Faubuses or the George Wallaces who were the oppressive keepers of the gate. It was my own people.

Then, during a luncheon at a Hadassah hospital, I sat next to the director, and we discussed the hospital's chaplaincy program.

"Do you have Reform and Conservative chaplains at the hospital?" I asked.

He looked at me quizzically. "Why would a Reform or Conservative Jew want to meet with a chaplain?"

Horrified, I stifled my response. Apparently, the director came from a different place from that of Henrietta Szold and the American Jewish women who founded Hadassah and continue to support its hospitals. Like many Israelis in 1998, the director put Jews into two categories: the Orthodox—who cared deeply about such matters as prayer, chaplaincy, and the Wall—and secular Jews, who couldn't care less.

Before my first trip to Israel, coworkers at the *Jewish Bulletin* told me how wonderful it was to be in a country where everyone was my religion. But when I looked around me, it seemed nobody was my religion. As I walked through the Old City, I saw Armenian Orthodox Christians, Roman Catholic monks, Muslims, and ultra-Orthodox Jewish men garbed in black and carrying cell phones. They could worship freely. Their rights were guaranteed. Mine were not. Later in Tel Aviv, I overheard a guide at the Museum of the

Diaspora* lecturing to European visitors and bashing ultra-Orthodox Jews: "If they wanted to be authentic, they would dress like the Bedouin, instead of like eighteenth-century Polish antisemites," she said. "Some people think the answer is Conservative and Reform. But they haven't been around very long and for all we know, they could wind up becoming branches of Christianity."

What? How could an Israeli guide at the Museum of the Jewish People know so little about Judaism? I wanted to interrupt her, but I held my tongue. However, I expressed my concern when I arrived home. "Thank God I'm an American Jew. Thank God I can pray the way I wish," I told my cantor as I prepared for my bat mitzvah at age fifty-five.

Shortly after my return, I had a dream that completely changed the focus of my bat mitzvah talk a few weeks later. In my dream, I was praying at the Western Wall with my tallit draped over my head when two men in black approached me angrily for praying in a manner they considered inappropriate.

Rallying all my Janet of the Ark chutzpah, I looked them straight in the eye and repeated the Hebrew National slogan, "I answer to a higher authority. My prayer is between me and *HaShem*" (God).

In an earlier life, it would have been easy for me to turn my back on the Wall and leave religion to the extremists. But I have come to see our people as an endangered species, and I'm willing to go to the Wall for religious rights, not only in this country but in Israel.

Yet demonizing the ultrareligious helps nobody. They have a lesson to teach us. We as a people value holiness. The word *sacrifice* means "to make holy." The ritual Temple sacrifices enabled our ancestors to separate the holy from the mundane and to make the mundane holy.

Today many women, and men, are celebrating the bat and bar mitzvahs they were denied at age thirteen. But it's not a gift open to everyone—even now. After my bat mitzvah, I wrote about my experience in the *Jewish Bulletin* and received two memorable notes. One was from a poet and teacher at Tel Aviv

---

*   The museum is now called ANU—Museum of the Jewish People in Tel Aviv.

University, my seatmate on my flight home from Israel. She had grown up in an Orthodox home in Rochester, New York.

"Congratulations on your bat mitzvah," she wrote. "I've never been bat mitzvah—my family was too religious."

The other was from a stranger. "Maybe, if enough adult women-of-valor also become daughters of the commandments," she wrote, "my husband will see that it's pointless to continue to forbid me to become a religiously adult Jew. Maybe..."

Maybe, indeed. And maybe, if enough adult women reclaim their voices as Jews, our sisters at the Wall will be able to sing, dance, and worship publicly with the *kavanah* (prayerful intention) of their brothers.

And now, for the rest of the story: that note I planted in the Wall. Did I honestly believe a miracle would happen? Was I talking to the Wall? Perhaps. In my mid-fifties, I knew it would take more than a note in the crack in a wall to find my intended.

I was reminded of that old story about Sammy, the elderly Jew who prays that he'll win the lottery. Every night he prays, "Dear God, make me a winner." But every morning when the winners are announced, he doesn't hear his name called.

In desperation, he calls upon God.

"Sammy," God entreats, "you gotta buy a ticket."

So I bought another ticket, so to speak. As 1999 approached, I made a New Year's resolution, and I placed another ad in the *Jewish Bulletin*.

CHAPTER 12

THE START OF SOMETHING BIG

1999

Once again, it was a new year, the last year of a millennium. For a haphazard gourmet like me, the kitchen seemed the logical place for a New Year's resolution, so I began the year by refinancing my townhouse and signing a contract for a kitchen remodel. I would reface the cat-marred cabinet doors from the previous owner, replace the cracked linoleum, and add a new range with two large burners along with an oven that could hold a full-sized cookie sheet. While it would never become a dream kitchen—the space in my townhouse was too small—the improvement would be immeasurable.

The kitchen was a beginning, but I had other goals. In January 1999, I made one last-ditch attempt to find Mr. Right. I wrote another singles ad, placing it online as well as in the *Jewish Bulletin*:

CUTE WRITER SEEKS leading man for long-playing drama.
Improvise, create sparkling dialogue, passionate interludes. Musical

ability a plus but no scene-throwers. I'm cute, slim, petite, 5'1",
stylish, extroverted, introspective, intellectual and occasionally out-
rageous. Great cook, cuddler, love outdoors, opera, travel. You're
49-60, active, healthy, ready for comeback after long-term mar-
riage. Willing to share marquee with woman your age, who looks
10-15 years younger. N/s, n/drugs.

At the time, I enjoyed a delicious long-distance correspondence with a baritone sax player who lived on a Southern California houseboat; we discussed
jazz chords and Jewish mysticism. At first, he seemed eager to meet me, but
then he got a dog named Lucy, which changed his availability. Then I had a
phone conversation with a man from Marin. He decided I was too old for him. I
decided he was too old for me. I had lunch with a man whose dyed-orange hair
stuck straight up. That was bad enough, but then he entertained me over mush-
room-stuffed crepes with sob stories about his problem children. I relayed the
experience to my friend Phyllis, who recalled an unpleasant lunch with the same
man. Their one-time date revolved around his hard-luck stories. "Don't go out
with anyone until you've checked with me first!" she advised, more than once.

I took Phyllis's message to heart. Since she had not dated a suave marketing
executive who moonlighted as a corporate entertainer, I auditioned him. We
had a lovely lunch at the California Café in Walnut Creek followed by a Gilbert
and Sullivan performance. We both enjoyed the operetta, and had much in
common, particularly our love of Broadway show tunes. I even lined him up
to sing duets with me at my synagogue's black-tie fundraiser.

I never expected I would be the one to break the date. After all, my mother
had always told me, "Never cancel a date—even if it's with girlfriends—because
something better comes along." I had passed those words on to my children,
and I stuck by them as if they were an eleventh commandment.

But shortly after my lunch with Mr. Suave, I received an intriguing email
from a man named Allen who didn't even subscribe to the *Jewish Bulletin*.

However, Pete Gordon, who rented the cottage behind Allen's house, did. When Pete was away, Allen picked up his mail, leafed through the *Bulletin*, and spotted my ad.

His response:

> From: anon.AKEEPER@personalspage.com
> Subject: 2good2btrue
>
> I love to sing duets, hike and bike, hug and talk, travel and explore. I'm a healthy, energetic 5'9" professional educator (I design and teach Continuing Ed. courses for EE's) who travels often, has green eyes, slim athletic build, and salt and pepper hair. I subscribe to Theatreworks, West Bay Opera, and S.F. MOMA. I love to bike, but I'm not a fanatic. I play softball every Sunday with my brother and friends.
>
> I sing bass in a chorus on Tuesdays, and my grandson and I play together every Thursday from 5 until 9. I like to eat, and often cook my own meals. I've been divorced 5 years, after a 25-year marriage. My life is full, but I miss having a spirited special someone in my life and would gladly make room. Call Allen or use their e-mail service, tho I hate to type.

As a brand-new grandma, I was impressed that Allen had a grandson. Plus, he was in a chorus, as was I, and he was a bass, not a temperamental tenor. But what the heck was an EE? Elementary educator?

I phoned Allen, who lived in Silicon Valley, where he was an electrical engineer, not a grade-school teacher. I lived in Alameda, on the other side of the bay. We were geographically incompatible, but we decided to meet in the middle, in San Francisco, where I had an alumni luncheon on a Saturday.

I suggested Macy's. He groaned. Letting me know he detested department stores, he suggested FAO Schwarz instead. At that time, a branch of the New

York toy store was on Stockton Street, across from Macy's.

"Legos or Raggedy Anns?" I asked.

"Legos," he responded assertively.

We exchanged photos. I sent him a picture of me with my then-newborn grandchild, Lindsay. He sent me two email photos, including one in which he was kicking up his heels in a cow costume. Then he sent me a cartoon about two people on a blind date who had sent one another old photos and waited at a restaurant in vain, wondering why the other hadn't shown up.

Understanding his concern, I sent him what I described as a "more-recent photo." Then I attached a JPEG of Golda Meir.

I arrived at FAO Schwarz before him, and I stood near the Legos, by the mat piano memorialized in *Big*, with Tom Hanks. When he rode up the escalator, he wasn't wearing a cow costume, but he was grinning broadly as he held up the photo of the late Israeli prime minister and looked around, ostensibly seeking a woman who resembled her.

After playing a duet of "Row, Row, Row Your Boat," tapping our feet on the piano, we walked up Grant Avenue. Since we were in Chinatown, I looked in several hardware stores for cooking chopsticks to replace my broken ones, but the ones in the windows were flimsy. Letting me know he had had that experience himself, he told me he would be glad to reinforce my cooking chopsticks, something he had done with his own. When we stopped for tea in a Chinatown bakery, he looked at me, saying, "You are cute! But Alameda?" He also let on that he was not eager to remarry but was interested in pursuing a relationship.

A week or so later, on a Sunday, I invited him to join me on a walk along the bay in Alameda. I just happened to have leftover Moroccan-style Rock Cornish game hen in apricot sauce that I just happened to have prepared the night before as well as the remains of a cinnamon coffeecake I had baked for a women's group that had met in my home that morning.

I didn't get out the fine china for lunch, and I didn't put flowers on the table. After all, that would have been too obvious.

CHAPTER 13

DO I DARE?

1999

What was I thinking? Not only was I inviting a stranger into my home on our second date, I was also feeding him. Was this entrapment? Was I obvious? Did he know I was harmless? Did I know he was harmless?

"My parents are concerned about you," I emailed Allen. "They wonder if you might be an ax murderer. Should I look up ax murderers on the web and see if your name is there?

"That won't be necessary," he said, supplying an alternative email address, with a bunch of slashes: allen@axmurderers.argh\\///

He arrived at my condo with no ax to grind. Instead, he carried a sprig of sweet-smelling daphne from his garden and even sweeter pastries from a Chinese bakery.

My "leftover" Moroccan game hen and coffeecake did not go unremarked, but he thought it was funny. Although I didn't know this at the time, when he opened the JPEG of Golda Meir, he had said to himself, "That she can cook is only alleged. But she does have a sense of humor."

After lunch, we walked along the lagoons toward the San Francisco Bay shoreline and returned along other lagoons as we encircled Bay Farm Island, where I lived. He was doing most of the talking, telling me about his family, his music, the company he started that had folded the previous summer. As a reporter, I was used to doing interviews, and I've mastered the art of interruption when an interviewee is talking on automatic pilot. Often, it's because they have a script: a book they're promoting, an episode they're recapitulating, a point they want to make. But that wasn't the case with Allen.

Finally, I looked at him and said, "Stop auditioning. You've got the part!"

He says that ever since then, I've been the one who has done most of the talking.

Meanwhile, as we continued our walk, he spied a shopping cart along the pathway and asked if the supermarket was nearby. It was, so as we continued our walk, he pushed the cart back to the Safeway parking lot.

Not only is this man a character, he has character, I said to myself, recalling the lessons imbedded into my psyche by my mother and by Mrs. Maglin, my eighth-grade homeroom and math teacher, who lectured us that in choosing a mate, character is so much more important than personality. Most of my classmates were bored, but I took her seriously—even when she said, "A lady doesn't chew gum, *ever.*" To this day, I don't chew gum, ever. Gummies and Jujyfruits are another story.

We returned to my townhouse and hopped into his car to attend a popular Brazilian film, *Central Station*. In the car, he sang along to his choir's recording of the Hebrew song "Bashana Haba'ah" ("Next Year"). Then he held my hand. I wasn't sure what his intentions were, but he certainly could sing.

After the movie, we stopped at a Chinese restaurant on Solano Avenue, between Berkeley and Albany. When the waiter came to take our order, Allen suddenly stopped talking to me.

"I don't like to treat servers as if they're invisible," he said, resuming our conversation after the waiter had left with our order.

Following dinner, we were walking with our arms around each other when we bumped into Marcia, from my women's group, who was with her husband, Ben. I introduced Allen, and they smiled knowingly. Marcia was thrilled that I had ostensibly moved on after Rex the Remote had broken my heart.

Later, Marcia said to me, "He's too good to be true."

Not only that, but my friend Phyllis hadn't gone out with him, another good sign.

Later, when I met his brother and his ninety-three-year-old mother, I was assured that Allen was indeed a keeper.

After our second date, five minutes after Allen left my condo, he phoned from the road. Was something the matter?

No, he just wanted to thank me for a wonderful day.

CHAPTER 14

THIS GUY'S IN LOVE WITH ME?

1999

Who is this guy? What could I possibly have in common with an electrical engineer in Silicon Valley? He lived in an upscale (650) area-code neighborhood while I lived in a condo in middle-rung East Bay (510). In the world of singles, he was G.U., geographically undesirable, not to mention O.U., occupationally unimaginable. But this guy loved theater and opera, and he could sing Cole Porter with panache. He was also a remarkable raconteur, charming the likes of Noël Coward in a bar in the Seychelles during a break in his Peace Corps service. But was he seducing me with his gift of gab, just as Noël had tried to seduce him? He said no to Noël. Would I say yes to him?

One thing we had in common: the 1990s had not been good years. After a difficult divorce and the loss of a company he started, Allen had managed to keep the house, buying out his ex and refinancing more than once.

"Those were tough times," he said, adding that he became Mr. Mom to two teenage girls.

Allen was no stranger to tough times. Born during the Depression to lower-middle-class parents in Wilmington, Delaware, he had carved his own way. When he was a University of Delaware sophomore, his father died suddenly of a heart attack at age forty-seven. His mother, Pearl, was the first American-born child of Rosa Israelowitz, a Romanian Jewish woman whose life was tarnished by tragedy. On the way to Palestine, she lost her first husband and two of her children to a typhus epidemic in Cyprus. With her one remaining son, she sailed for America, where she was swiftly married off to a much older widower with children of his own. The message she passed on to her daughter: "You make the best of it."

Pearl was a brilliant student, but her father forced her into a commercial program despite her teacher's pleadings. She married Ben Weissberg in 1927 and gave birth to Jerry, a year later. When Jerry was about two, Pearl divorced Ben, and the two grandmothers took Jerry's care into their own hands. Pearl, posing as a single woman, left for Wilmington, where her brother had settled. She had no difficulty finding a job as a secretary and office manager. She also found a husband, Albert. When they first married, Albert did not know about Jerry's existence. Allen, who grew up as an only child, met Jerry around the time of his bar mitzvah.

After Albert's sudden death, Allen's distraught mother swiftly sold everything she could and moved into an inexpensive apartment. Allen supported himself by working in his fraternity house.

A summer job at CGS in Connecticut changed Allen's life. Owner Carl Sontheimer, who later gained acclaim as the creator of the original Cuisinart food processor, became Allen's mentor and lifelong friend. Sontheimer and the CGS engineers helped Allen transfer to Cornell, where he was the first student to earn a five-year degree in electrical engineering and solid-state physics. He and Sontheimer went into business together, manufacturing products that Allen had created as senior projects at Cornell.

Allen later left for UC Berkeley to complete his doctorate, but after a year, he joined the Peace Corps, building roads and teaching electronics in Tanzania. After he returned to Connecticut, he married his former Berkeley girlfriend and they settled later in Silicon Valley, where their two daughters were born. Ever energetic, Allen tried three Silicon Valley companies before he launched Pacific Monolithics, which produced complex integrated circuits used in satellite receivers and Wi-Fi components.

In 1993, his first wife left him. Five years later, Pacific Monolithics went belly-up, leaving him with a stock certificate worth $7.37 and eight folding chairs purchased at auction.

What we had in common was the sudden loss of a mate, the loss of a job, and the loss of a dream. For me, when the *Oakland Tribune* was sold in 1992, just as I turned fifty, I was emotionally wiped out, took a job I hated, became depressed, and kvetched for the better part of a year. Allen, by contrast, was not bitter. "I'm not wired that way," he says.

When I met him, he was teaching engineering professionals in short courses throughout the world. Allen was not risk averse, but he was not particularly eager to marry again. I was a bit gun-shy myself.

CHAPTER 15

'WHO IS GONNA BE DESSERT?'*

Presidents' Day, 1999

The Friday after our all-day date, I received an email while I was at work: "If I can get out of my blind date for tonight, can I join you at services in Alameda?"

This from a man who probably hadn't gone to synagogue since his bar mitzvah.

This from a man who hadn't dated a Jewish woman since the 1960s, when he was in the Peace Corps—"if you can call that dating," he said later.

What was I supposed to say? I didn't approve of breaking dates. I remembered my experience with Josh the Jerk, who kept a woman waiting outside a movie theater while I was with him. On the other hand . . .

In any case, Allen broke the date and arrived at my doorstep wearing a coat and tie—certainly out of character—and we walked to the Chinese restaurant

---

*   "You Are Woman, I Am Man," *Funny Girl.*

for dinner before heading to services at the far end of the shopping center. Allen calls himself an atheist, but he is also a pragmatist who figured the way to a woman's heart was through her temple.

That said, he read Hebrew far better than I did, and he certainly knew how to chant. Later he told me that when he celebrated his bar mitzvah, the rabbi told him he would make a good cantor, but Allen saw his talents in another direction. Namely, hardware. When he was still in a crib, he said he preferred adult-sized nuts, bolts, and washers to rattles and Tinkertoys. At age seven, he was taking apart working radios. Sometimes, he put them together again.

"It drove my father crazy!" he said.

When he was nine or ten, a cousin gave him a kit that consisted of a bag of parts, a schematic diagram—no step-by-step instructions—and a chassis with holes.

"I made a radio," he said.

But this was information I found out later, long after he was fixing everything in sight in my townhouse. However, he did no such thing on our third date. For one, it was Shabbat, when you're not supposed to work. For another, he was focused on wooing me.

After services, we stood outside my townhouse looking at the moon. "You know we're going to spend the rest of our lives together," he pronounced.

What? I knew no such thing, but I was flattered.

Then he made a proposal, of sorts: "Come live with me. We'll move to San Francisco."

Wait! I'd heard that song before—wasn't it supposed to be Boston, Denver, LA? But I wasn't interested in moving. For one, I was about to remodel my kitchen. For another, I loved living by the waterways in Alameda in a place of my own. I wanted a partner, but I certainly didn't want to be uprooted, particularly now that I had a nice community of friends in my synagogue, and work was just an easy bus or ferry ride away.

The next day, I flew to Southern California to visit both my daughter's family in San Diego and my parents, who were staying in Orange County. While I was at my parents' place—I didn't have a mobile phone at the time, and my parents did not have an internet connection—Allen phoned several times, prompting my father to say, "He's obviously crazy about you."

Later at my daughter's house, I received repeated emails from Allen. Meanwhile, John, my son-in-law, said, "Hey, Janet, I hear you have a new squeeze."

I showed him the picture of Allen kicking up his heels on Halloween in his unflattering cow costume.

"Nice!" he said.

With Allen in hot pursuit, what was I going to do about the professional entertainer whom I had asked to escort me to my synagogue's fundraiser? It was just three weeks away. Short of illness or a death in the family, I didn't break dates, but I needed to consider other factors. By escorting me on a Saturday night, the entertainer would be giving up a potential moneymaking gig. Was it fair to him? Was I ready for an exclusive relationship? Where was I going?

I wrote to the entertainer, headlining the email, "A very hard note to write." In the email, I let him know that I was becoming involved with someone else and, under the circumstances, I didn't feel right asking him to turn down business on my account. However, I left the decision in his hands.

He responded graciously: "Good luck with your new love."

When I returned from Southern California on Presidents' Day, I had a couple of messages on my home phone. One was from a former *Tribune* colleague, telling me that a coworker whom I often met for lunch had taken a fall and was found dead in his home. Another was from Allen. He was staying in a San Francisco hotel while attending a technical society symposium. We could have dinner . . . and would I spend the night?

Was I gonna be dessert? I wasn't ready for this. I phoned my friend Mary, peppering my conversation with obscenities. *What the f--- was I supposed to do?* I was quite upset about the death of my former coworker, and was hardly in the mood for romance, not even with a guy in a cow suit. Mary became angry with me, telling me to calm down and stop cussing.

Yes, I was frightened. I hadn't been with a man in more than a year. I didn't like my body. I didn't like much of anything about me. But I knew that sooner or later, we would be getting together. I recalled that wonderful scene in *Funny Girl*, when gambler Nicky Arnstein (Omar Sharif) invites Fanny Brice (Barbra Streisand) to dine in a private room, enticing her with *boeuf bordelaise*.

It would take more than a fancy meal to entice me, I told Allen. "What's more, I have a fat tush."

He responded, matter-of-factly, "I know that."

Was that supposed to reassure me?

"I know a nice restaurant," he said. "We'll talk."

I packed a small bag and took BART to the city. Allen met me at the station. We had a lovely dinner at a restaurant south of Market Street—no, the room wasn't private, and I didn't order *boeuf bordelaise*. Roast duck à l'orange is more my style. We talked through our concerns as we walked to his hotel.

The next morning, he told me, "I think I'm falling in love with you." Then he fainted in the shower. Low blood pressure, he explained. Was this what I was signing up for?

The following weekend, I joined him in Palo Alto, where he had tickets to *Carmen* at West Bay Opera. On Saturday, I met his ninety-two-year-old mother, who was living at a board-and-care home. I gave her a picture of me with my infant granddaughter, Lindsay. She was thrilled that Allen's new girl-friend was Jewish. Allen wept when he left her; after a couple of strokes, she wasn't the woman she had been. But she was his last link to the past. I also met his brother, Jerry, who lived nearby and came over to Allen's house every Sunday, bringing bagels, along with stories of his life in Brooklyn and his time in an orphanage, when aging relatives couldn't take care of him. As adults, Allen and Jerry became real brothers.

Not long after meeting Jerry, I met the rest of Allen's family, and my parents flew in from Orange County to celebrate Passover with all of us. Allen passed the parent test. However, his house did not. It had a dark living room that nobody used, and an even darker family room suitable only for watching TV at night.

My mother's pronouncement: "It has a nice backyard," she said, "but I wouldn't want to live there. I like where you live now."

So did I. Allen's home had too many steps between the bedroom and the bathroom. The garden needed work. The driveway was broken up and the entrance was uninviting. More than once, I drove right past the house because it lacked a welcoming face. When I did find the entrance, I was stabbed by a prickly plant.

Sadly, my mother never lived to see how I made Allen's house mine.

CHAPTER 16

SO WHEN ARE YOU GETTING ENGAGED?

There is a tide in the affairs of men
Which taken at the flood, leads on to fortune;
Omitted, all the voyage of their life
is bound in shallows and in miseries.
On such a full sea are we now afloat,
And we must take the current when it serves,
Or lose our ventures.
—WILLIAM SHAKESPEARE, *JULIUS CAESAR,*
ACT 4, SCENE 3

Summer 1999

During my kitchen remodel in Alameda, while adding new outlets and revising some of the electrical work, Allen proposed to me. It was an oblique, between-the-lines proposal.

"But you won't be living here long!" he said, adding another outlet.

"What do you mean?"

"What I mean is, you'll be living with me."

"Is that a proposal or a proposition?"

He hesitated. "It's a proposal, I guess. Will you marry me?"

I hesitated. "Eventually," I said.

He looked crestfallen.

"What should I have said?" I asked.

"Yes, but not right away."

"Okay, if that sounds better to you, 'Yes, but not right away.'"

Why did Allen, who had said he was not interested in getting married again, suddenly change his tune?

"The commute was deadly," he quipped.

Although we lived only about thirty-five miles apart, on a Friday evening at rush hour, driving across the Dumbarton Bridge from Palo Alto and then negotiating I-880 to Alameda could take as long as two hours. Plus, in 1999 our phone bills across two area codes were outrageous. The calls were clocked at long-distance rates.

Yes, the commute was inconvenient for him, but why should I be the one to move? Seven years after my life fell apart when the *Oakland Tribune* died, I now owned my own townhouse in a dream community surrounded by water. Just over the bridge was the main island of Alameda, with funky antique shops, Victorian homes once owned by sea captains, and cute cottages reminiscent of Andy Griffith's Mayberry, and across the estuary was Oakland. I could commute to my job in San Francisco taking a short bus ride or a ferry. I could walk to the supermarket, the synagogue, a Chinese restaurant, or aerobics classes. More to the point, I had friends. Why would I want to move to Silicon Valley, where I knew nobody?

Allen had done his homework, and he had lined up his talking points. Not only was his work in Silicon Valley, but his entire family lived there: his mother, daughters, grandson, brother, niece, and nephew. If I moved to Silicon Valley, I could commute to San Francisco by Caltrain and board a bus or shuttle to work from the train station. It wasn't as convenient as hopping on just one bus or as scenic as ferrying across the bay, but it was doable. Besides, he pointed out, he had a better kitchen.

That said, I wasn't ready, so we didn't get engaged. But I was in my midfifties. Allen was sixty-one. Eventually, I would have to decide. I loved Allen, I wanted to marry Allen, but I didn't want to move.

My friend Judy's husband, Walt, a Realtor, set me straight. Houses, he said, are expendable. Relationships are not.

I had a choice: Allen or Alameda.

Alameda or Allen?

I couldn't hold onto both.

"When are you getting engaged?" friends and coworkers asked.

"I'm not!" I responded.

"So, you're not serious?"

"We're having too much fun to be serious."

"Well, be serious for a minute."

"If we set a date, I will tell you when. I will invite you to the wedding, but I will not get engaged."

"Why not?"

"Because it's a jinx," I said. "Allen and his former fiancée were engaged for quite a while, with no real intention to marry, so what's the point of getting engaged?"

"Does that mean you won't get a ring?"

"Allen's fiancée received a ring. I don't need another ring, and I certainly don't want hers."

"Aren't you cheating yourself out of a diamond?"

"What do I need a diamond for?"

"So what's the story? Are you getting married?"

"I'll let you know."

"Well, if you marry Allen, all of us are gonna be the bridesmaids," said Judy, discussing her plans for those in my women's group. "We'll wear matching dresses, from Mervyn's," a former midscale department store where Judy was unlikely to shop for anything more serious than a bathmat.

"Okay, but no matching dresses. Promise me?"

"It's a deal."

The rabbi approached me one Shabbat after services. He had heard rumors. Since he would be the one to officiate, he had to know *if* and *when*. By that time, summer was nearly over, and as we approached the High Holidays, a fall wedding was out of the question. That left winter. The rainy season. My parents were scheduled to rent a house in Southern California in February, which seemed like a good time. We settled on February 13, *erev* (the day before) Valentine's Day. Allen would be teaching a course in Nice later that month, and a honeymoon in Provence sounded delectable.

We met with the rabbi, who asked us why we wanted to get married. After all, we were both at midlife, we weren't going to have children, and nobody was pressuring us to make our relationship legal.

I thought for a minute. "Because life is short, and Allen makes me smile."

I recalled our summer backpacking trip, when we traipsed into the middle of the redwoods to set up camp, only to discover that the tent poles were still in the car.

Ever the engineer, Allen rigged up a solution, using rope and tree branches. It worked, more or less. Then the next morning, on our way back from the outhouse, we were stopped in midtrack by a couple of Roosevelt elk that were noshing through the ferns surrounding our campsite. We were in their fern bar, and they weren't about to move. Improvising again, Allen stood atop the bear box, placing a banana in the middle of his forehead in an attempt to intimidate the elk. I was laughing hysterically and trying to take pictures of a ridiculous man with a banana on his head. But when the six-point bull elk began shuffling his feet, Allen realized he was the trespasser. Fortunately, the elk moved on and we were able to prepare our breakfast rather than being breakfast.

In addition to being more than slightly goofy, Allen approaches life with a song, and I sing along. Even though sopranos normally take the melody, in this relationship, I do the harmony—and it has worked. Whatever happens, there's a song to be sung: Gilbert and Sullivan, Frank Sinatra, the Beatles. Years ago, my mother told me that Allen's impromptu vocal outbursts embarrassed my daughter and her husband, and I needed to talk to him about that. "What's more," she said, "by singing along, you're encouraging him."

"Mom, have you heard of the play *I Love You, You're Perfect, Now Change*? This is Allen, and this is the Allen I love. Because of who he is, my life has become more joyful. No, I wouldn't dream of changing him."

I wanted a small wedding, in the rabbi's study. No big deal. Allen wanted nothing of the sort. He wanted his forty-voice choir, the Aurora Singers, to sing during the ceremony. He had even picked out the music.

My mother couldn't believe it.

"He didn't really ask the entire choir to sing at the wedding?" my mother asked more than once.

"Yes, and the June Taylor Dancers," I quipped. "Unfortunately, he couldn't get the Mormon Tabernacle Choir."

"Is that what you want?"

"This is what he wants. These are his friends. They helped him through a difficult divorce, and he wants to include them."

The small wedding I had envisioned had now grown to close to two hundred guests, twice as many as my first wedding, ten times the number that attended Allen's previous wedding in a friend's living room. It was an affair to remember.

CHAPTER 17

GRANNY JANNY AND GRAMPY GET MARRIED

2000

*B*efore my first marriage, I was adamant about the music. I absolutely did not want to march to "Here Comes the Bride." Not only was it a cliché, it was also Richard Wagner's greatest hit. Why was an antisemite's march acceptable at the wedding of a Jewish bride? But while I was on the phone discussing my preferences with the music director, who happened to be my former piano teacher, my father picked up an extension and said, "I'm paying for it, and I want 'Here Comes the Bride.'" Had I been a bigger brat, I might have said, "Okay, then you walk down the aisle by yourself, Dad, because I'm going to turn on my heels." But that was then.

In 1965, my wedding—like that of many upper-middle-class Jewish brides—was a parents' affair. I had some input. I chose the venue and the flowers. I was also able to invite the friends I wanted, which was more than some of my friends were allowed to do. But most of the guests, besides family members, were longtime friends of my parents. Because my non-Jewish ex was from Detroit and his family members were mostly Midwestern Protestants, only a handful of guests from the groom's side attended. Some invitees didn't understand protocol for a sit-down wedding reception, and we experienced culture clash. One rural aunt's RSVP, mailed well after the venue's deadline, was, "We're not sure if my husband can get the time off, but if we do come, there will be four of us."

My father went ballistic and phoned the groom's parents. "Maybe" is not an acceptable RSVP for a luncheon at a Manhattan hotel. In fact, "maybe" is a non-RSVP for any invitation. As it turned out, they didn't come.

Those headaches, however, were more of an annoyance to my parents than to me. Young brides at that time tolerated parental takeovers of their weddings for two reasons: the parents wrote the checks, and so did their guests. In the early 1960s, couples in grad school could live quite well on the proceeds from their weddings. In our case, the monetary wedding gifts covered the cost of the furniture for our first post-grad-school apartment. In fact, the Lane bedroom suite and Founders oil walnut dining room table from Detroit's J. L. Hudson (now defunct) are now ensconced in the Silicon Valley home where I live with Allen. A couple of years ago, we refinished the table and re-caned the chairs. The Lane bedroom furniture suite needs work. It will always need work.

Fast-forward to my second wedding in 2000. All the decisions were ours, along with the bills, and money was tight for both of us. Allen was paying alimony, and I had been living on a shoestring for years. After searching for months for an appropriate second-wedding dress, I finally found a simple ivory gown for $125 on a rack in Macy's junior department. My friend Mary and her daughter, Ida, made me a small tiara with pearls. Finding comfortable flats to match my ivory gown cost me close to one hundred dollars at Nordstrom since they had to be dyed. I schlepped all over the Bay Area before I found a wedding cake that suited us—not too sweet and not too frilly—but I hope I never have to taste another buttercream rose.

Meanwhile, Marcia and Ben, who had won the use of the social hall at a synagogue auction, donated the hall to us. Marcia enlisted the women's group to decorate the tables with small flowers she had purchased at a wholesale market. We shared the cost of the sanctuary flowers with a bar mitzvah family. Instead of bouquets, my women's group members each carried a single white rose, and my daughter and I carried single calla lilies, recalling my mother's 1939 wedding picture. Instead of matching bridesmaids' dresses, they each wore a blue-green dress of their choice.

On the nights my women's group met in the synagogue library, I would hear Dave Altschuler's band practicing upbeat dance music, and I'd stop to listen on the way out. One night during my year of bleak, they were playing "After the Lovin'," a romantic ballad popularized by Engelbert Humperdinck. I ran out of the synagogue in tears. Then I hired Dave's band to play at our reception. When he asked for requests, "After the Lovin'" was at the top.

"Now you will have happy associations with this song," he said.

The temple sisterhood did the catering, providing the food at cost. Beverages were wine, beer, and nonalcoholic drinks, not hard liquor, as was the case at my first wedding. However, the sisterhood folks placed the champagne in the freezer to cool it—and left it there too long.

February 13, 2000—our wedding day—did not start out auspiciously. Northern California was in the middle of La Niña, the cold phase following El Niño the year before, and the town of Alameda was flooded. In fact, we found out later that the social hall where our reception was held also flooded, but nobody told us until later. We began the day in my townhouse with a bagel-and-coffee breakfast. For whatever reason, I was still hemming and ironing my dress, and then I ironed my younger stepdaughter's.

The morning of the wedding, we placed a one-page mock *Jewish Bulletin* on every chair in the sanctuary, headlined "It's a miracle! A match made in newsprint." The mock newspaper told the story of how Allen and I met, along with photos of Allen kicking up his heels in his cow costume, me with newborn Lindsay in my arms, and Golda Meir, who brought us together. *Bulletin* art director Cathleen Maclearie designed the piece, and I wrote the story, using the name of my "altar ego," Tiffany Lipschitz, Society Editor.

The lede: "Defying the odds, a *Jewish Bulletin* copy editor who is over 50 is marrying a man whom she met through a *Bulletin* personals ad—without lying about her age."

This wedding was 100 percent ours. My seventeen-month-old granddaughter, Lindsay, carried flowers in a tiny basket, dropping them all at once as she walked down the aisle with my daughter. Tim (not his real name), age four, carried a small unicorn with the wedding rings basted onto the horn. Allen was escorted by his daughter. Our brothers followed, and I walked between my parents, as is the traditional Jewish custom. We did not follow that custom at my first wedding, which was conducted by a Unitarian pastor and was more in the mainstream American tradition.

As we walked down the aisle, the Aurora Singers sang "Bashana Haba'ah," the Hebrew song Allen had wooed me with in the car on our second date. When we stood under the chuppah (marriage canopy), the rabbi recited the marriage blessings, the cantor chanted them, and the choir sang Denes Agay's arrangement of "The Old Irish Blessing." Its words are rooted in the Hebrew priestly benediction from the book of Numbers.

I was supposed to encircle Allen either three times or seven times, both measures of good luck. I accidentally encircled him four times, but nobody was counting. What else? I had bought Allen a lovely blue-green tie to coordinate with my bridesmaids' dresses, but he left it in Palo Alto. Instead, he wore the only tie he had brought with him, a black-and-silver print flocked with tiny Donalds, Mickeys, and Goofys. I had bought him that tie for Hanukkah because he had asked for a goofy tie. Symbolic? Guests couldn't see the Disney characters unless they looked closely. People looked only if I told them to, and they laughed.

Meanwhile, Tim, wearing a three-piece mint-green tuxedo, stood under the chuppah taking his jacket on and off and grinning. Allen's brother, Jerry, tried to keep him under control. In honor of Allen's proclivity for wordplay, which his older daughter shares, I added my own unscripted vow: I promised to become fluent in the "Allenese" language, and never take my husband "for granite." Allen, in turn, promised to lead me "on a merry chase . . . fix whatever is broken, pick up after [himself] and try not to fix things that are working."

The rabbi, who compared Allen and me to teenagers in love, departed from tradition to allow each of us to shatter a wine glass, followed by choruses of "Siman Tov U'Mazal Tov" ("good signs and good luck").

This was the first Jewish wedding for each of us. Some of the customs we incorporated harked back to older traditions, and some were new. Instead of a receiving line after the ceremony itself, Allen and I were ushered into the synagogue library for some alone time, with two burly friends guarding the door so nobody could enter. In times past, this custom, called *yichud*, enabled bride and groom, who previously had never touched or been alone together, to consummate their marriage. Fat chance! Consummating a marriage on a hard oak library table would have been difficult enough had we been forty years younger. But innocence was not something we could claim, particularly since we'd spent the night before our wedding in bed, with our grandson between us. A new premarital custom?

During the toasts, Kara from my women's group talked about the miracle of my meeting Allen at midlife, and *Bulletin* editor and publisher Marc Klein announced to the crowd that Allen had met me through an ad in the newspaper he didn't even spend seventy-five cents for. Allen reached into his pocket and offered to give Marc three quarters, not a bad bride price.

For me, one of the thrills was seeing my parents dance together, knowing that perhaps it would be the last time they would have the opportunity as my father had terminal cancer. Cathleen Maclearie, who took pictures, made sure she snapped plenty of my parents. As at all Jewish weddings, the band played "Sunrise, Sunset," and there were tears amid the joy.

Since my parents were staying at my townhouse, and Allen and I didn't want to spend our wedding night with my parents in the next room, we booked a

Victorian B&B in Alameda. But the rain never stopped, and we sloshed our way to the inn. A prophetic beginning?

When I married the first time on a sunny summer day, I was told, "Blessed is the bride the sun shines on." So much for that! If the weather is foul, the prophecy is that the rain symbolizes tears of woe the bride will shed during her marriage. Others say rain symbolizes fertility—a bit late for us.

But I prefer my friend Mary's interpretation: the raindrops, she says, are the tears of joy shed because the angels are so happy. That works for us.

PART II

THE MERRY CHASE

CHAPTER 18

MISADVENTURE

1999–2019

When Allen recited his vows under the chuppah at Temple Israel, he promised me a merry chase, and I jumped aboard for the journey. During the first twenty years of our marriage, we'd journeyed to Europe multiple times as well as to South America, Southeast Asia, and Africa. Wherever we were, we drew adventure, and when things went awry, we had a story:

Barcelona: To Catch a Thief

OCTOBER 1999

On a Saturday in Barcelona, where Allen was teaching a one-week course a few months before our wedding, we were meandering through the Old City when a young man suddenly wrenched my purse off my shoulder.

Shouting, "Stop! Thief," Allen ran after the purse-snatcher in a chase out of Hitchcock.

Then, just as the thief was about to enter a tunnel and retrieve his bicycle, residents of the Old City blocked his way. He dropped the purse, and I burst into tears. What I remember most about Barcelona is not the Gaudi architecture, the museums, or the churches, but crazy Allen chasing madly after a man of maybe twenty-five and the locals rallying to help us.

Wrote Allen in an email: *He won't mess with 61-year-old Gringos again. The people who helped us in the chase were very solicitous. I was very hoarse for four days. Janet says I may laugh at her bizarre money belt, but the purse only contained a camera, eyeglasses, makeup, and hidden tissues. Imagine that thief, panting and shaking, dumping out the contents of the purse, with its secret compartments only to find not a peseta as reward for his persistence. Well, he could have used the tissues.*

A couple of days later, we took the train to Tarragona because the infrequent train to Girona, where we really wanted to go, had just left. When we arrived in Tarragona, we discovered everything was closed because it was a local holiday. All we could do was walk around the Roman ruins and peer at the cathedral from the outside. Suddenly, as we were circling the ruins, we spotted an English couple we had seen the day before at the monastery in Montserrat. At that time, I had told Allen that the bearded man must be an Oxford professor, as he was wearing a well-aged tweed jacket, red socks, and a tartan tie, and he carried a dog-eared tour book. He turned out to be Anthony Bryer, a noted historian and founder of the University of Birmingham's Centre for Byzantine Studies. His much more conventionally dressed wife, Jenny, was a retired French teacher.

Bryer, whose wife called him by his surname, was also disappointed that Tarragona seemed to be shuttered, but he offered another suggestion: Poblet, home of a working twelfth-century Cistercian monastery and a UNESCO World Heritage site, was about thirty miles away. Would we split the cost of a cab ride? We agreed.

We entered the monastery without a tour guide, taking in the stunning

Gothic cloisters and statuary as well as the royal tombs. As we awaited our cab for our return trip to Tarragona, we chatted over beer. Bryer shared his experiences growing up in Jerusalem when it was under British rule. His mother had read children's stories on the radio there. Later in an email, he told us she had been a spy.

Over the course of our conversation, Allen discussed his Peace Corps service in Africa, recalling a disastrous formal tea party at the home of the governor general of the Seychelles. While seated in the stunning salon, Allen sneezed and sent his bone china teacup flying into the grand piano. Trying to grab it in midair, he wound up stomping on the saucer, imbedding crumbs into the Persian carpet. He told the Bryers that he had shared that story over drinks with a prominent guest at the hotel: English playwright Noël Coward, who propositioned him.

"When was that?" Jenny Bryer piped up.

Allen noted the dates.

She nodded. "He was quite ill then. That makes sense," she said, adding that the University of Birmingham research library had an extensive Noël Coward collection, including unpublished material.

When we returned home, we received an email about Coward's journals from his time in the Seychelles. He did not refer to Allen by name, but he did mention that he enjoyed looking out his window watching a couple of "half-naked Americans cavorting on the beach." How much cavorting Allen and his roommate did is an open question. For the record, Allen did not take Coward up on his offer—although he did let him know he would think about it. As far as our conversation with the Bryers, Allen wrote: *He and his wife really knew their ruins, and we traded stories from all over the world. A jolly good day.*

We sent the Bryers a note after our wedding, along with a picture. Sadly, Anthony Bryer, who was just a few months older than Allen, passed away in 2016. Noël Coward died in 1973 at age seventy-three. *The New York Times* obituary singled out Coward's "light sharp wit [that] had enlivened the English stage for half a century as actor, playwright, songwriter, composer and director." The obituary said that "the urbane Sir Noël gave the world unstintingly of what he called 'a talent to amuse.'" It made no mention of half-naked Americans. Nor did it mention that years after meeting Coward, an unnamed Peace Corps veteran-turned-engineer sharpened his talents as a singer, raconteur, and memoirist.

Lyon: A Traboule, Three Keys, and a Squatter Soirée
NOVEMBER 1999

From Barcelona, we traveled to Lyon, where my son, then twenty-seven, was editing an alternative journal. He was staying rent-free in an eighteenth-century building in the city center, with a view of the ballroom in the ostentatious city hall.

He and his former girlfriend from Australia shared a life that was straight out of *La Bohème*, relishing every minute of it, particularly their creative cuisine. They dined on vegetables that the purveyors had discarded. His greatcoat, purchased at a thrift store, looked like something Ebenezer Scrooge might have worn. Their combination shower and toilet, which we did not use, was just off the kitchen.

My son booked us in what was billed as a two-star hotel, but that was a stretch. Entering our room required three keys: one to navigate the secret passageway, known as a *traboule*, and then open the gate to a dark, squalid courtyard; another to enter another building that housed the hotel; and a third to get into the room itself, where there was barely room for us and the tiny TV, mounted above the bed. We watched *Law and Order* in French.

But the highlight of that trip was the potluck, held in an apartment across the hall from my son's. At the potluck, everybody brought a vegetarian dish, mostly in chipped pottery. When I asked for a *serviette* (napkin), my son gave me a dirty

look, and some of the attendees giggled or sneered. *Honestly, these Americans!*
Here is Allen's description:

> *We arrived late in Lyon and discovered the inspiration for the set*
> *of Rent. Someone from the show must have visited Janet's son and*
> *immortalized his and his neighbor's digs. That evening, we went*
> *to a squatter's soirée and potluck. This was not to be missed as a*
> *slice of Lyonnais life. I'm sure that this will make all the "in" travel*
> *books, certainly Europe on Five Francs a Day. Amazing what you*
> *can eat without recognizable flatware and dishes. The only thing*
> *that missed double duty was a Frisbee. Indeed, the POT-luck lived*
> *up to its billing, and luckily, the vegan food was quite edible, served*
> *up on a very low table, with the eaters either sitting on pillows, or*
> *more appropriately, squatting.*

The next day, I was enjoying morning coffee in Lyon's Old Town when Allen excused himself to use the facilities. An attractive fair-haired woman of a certain age, sitting at an adjoining table, smiled at me. Her name was Régine, and she taught English in a correspondence class. Would I be so kind as to look over her curriculum? I found a couple of grammatical errors, but since she didn't prepare the materials herself, she would have to live with the mistakes, as well as her own regrets.

Régine reached into her purse and pulled out a musty handkerchief embroidered with tiny flowers in the Japanese manner. Then she showed me her scrapbook filled with letters from her lover, a Japanese artist, or was he a poet? He had returned to Japan, and the letters had stopped. She believed he had died, but she continued to carry his memories in her portable scrapbook. Her story begged to be sung by Édith Piaf, perhaps, or a smoky-voiced chanteuse. When my husband returned, we went off to explore Lyon, carrying the memory of Régine with us.

Flying High, Flying Low
2000–2022

For many years, we carried our luggage onto the plane and weighed everything carefully, measuring the dimensions of our bags. But miscalculations happen. Returning from Ireland to Scotland via Ryanair, I was told my suitcase was well under the weight limit, but Allen's was a fraction of a kilogram over. The checker would not allow us to combine the weights. With passengers lined up behind us, Allen opened his suitcase, took out a heavy pair of hiking boots, and put them on. Then he took off his sneakers and stuffed them into his bag. The checker was furious, but with people waiting to board, she let us go. They say Ryanair charges customers to use the toilet. It's not true, but they certainly go out of their way to turn a short flight into a calamity.

Budget airlines often operate out of budget airports. Take Frankfurt-Hahn, a former US Army base about seventy-five miles from Frankfurt, Germany, and equidistant from Luxembourg. Arriving at the airport the evening before our flight, we saw signs posted for rental car returns, but we couldn't find anyone on duty. We bumped into a frantic American woman who was flying out that evening. How should she return her car? We shrugged. On a hunch, we parked the car and wheeled our suitcases into the terminal, where we found a rental car agent and turned in the keys.

Yes, that was what we were supposed to do. But how were we to know? As Allen frequently says during moments of frustration, "Next time we'll know."

Next time we'll also know not to book ourselves into a youth hostel that markets itself as an airport hotel. We had chosen the place because it was only two kilometers from the airport and offered free shuttle service. However, when we phoned, the night porter was the only one on duty, and he could not pick us up right away, so we waited at the airport bar. And waited. I sent out emails on a German computer with an inscrutable keyboard, and I was charged by the minute. At around 10:00 p.m., the night porter showed up and drove us to the hostel, only to tell us that it was cash only, but we were out of euros.

The porter dropped me off at the hostel, along with our suitcases and backpacks. He told me that the room was on the second floor, and it was the third door on the left, number ten. He handed me an oversized key. Then he and Allen got back into the car in search of an ATM, leaving me to find the actual room. There were no numbers on the doors, and the door third from the left on the second floor didn't open.

Aha, I said to myself. The European second floor was the third floor, in American speak, so I lugged the suitcases up another flight of stairs, put the key in the third door on the left, and miraculously, it opened. The room was well equipped—for a university student—with minimalist plank beds and stark wooden desks. There were even teabags for making a bare-bones breakfast, but hunger was not my priority.

When Allen returned, he was astonished that I had found the room and had managed to lug the suitcases up two flights. Somehow, we managed to get about five hours of sleep before boarding the hotel's shuttle for a 6:15 a.m. flight to London's Stansted Airport. With several hours until our return flight to the US via Heathrow, we decided to ride the airport bus into Central London.

I love London, but we hadn't banked on a two-hour ride to town during rush hour. Parking our suitcases at the hotel where we had stayed earlier that month, we did some last-minute shopping—Marks and Spencer shortbread is always on my list, along with artisan chocolate and tea. Allowing plenty of time, we reclaimed our suitcases at our hotel near Hyde Park before waiting for the big red double-decker that would take us to Paddington Station and the express train to Heathrow. The friendly bus conductor at the back of the bus helped me on with my bag, but the bus driver at the front took off before Allen boarded. Caught in an Oxford Street traffic jam, the bus moved slowly. Two blocks later, a huffing and puffing Allen caught up with the bus and leaped on, dragging his bags behind him.

Unfortunately, our flight home was through Chicago O'Hare, where the international and domestic terminals are far apart. But before we could make the journey from one terminal to the other, the inspectors stopped us. The agriculture folks confiscated two Hungarian salamis given to us by our son-in-law's grandparents. No meat allowed. Not fresh, dried, canned, or processed. Next time we'll know.

Finally, we made our way to the tram for the domestic terminal. This time, Allen hopped on board just as the doors were closing, leaving me in the dust.

When we travel to England, we often fly in and out of Manchester because it's less frenetic than Heathrow. However, it's the only terminal I know of where lipstick is treated as a liquid. Because I couldn't fit my lipsticks into my one-quart plastic bag, Allen and I did some reshuffling while we were in the queue. When the inspector saw lipsticks in Allen's near-empty plastic bag, he raised his eyebrows.

"Are these yours?" he said to Allen.

Allen winked.

The purple electric kettle we had purchased in Manchester received an even deeper level of scrutiny. To save space in his suitcase, Allen had stuffed the kettle with socks and underwear, which the inspector made him remove. As Allen aired his dirty laundry before dozens of frustrated travelers in the queue, all we could do was laugh.

Czechmate

2004

After Lyon, my son moved to Prague. He was living with a lovely woman from Yorkshire who later became his wife. Their lodgings were flexible. Sometimes they shared a circus wagon in an apple orchard. Fortunately, when we visited, they were living in a borrowed apartment, which was many steps up from the Lyonnais squat. Our trip at this leg of our journey was relatively uneventful, until the four of us decided to spend a weekend in Karlovy Vary (formerly Carlsbad), a spa town on the German border straight out of *Last Year at Marienbad*. Filled with crumbling rococo buildings and fading grand hotels, Karlovy Vary offered us a taste of another time, when those in search of a cure took the waters. We arrived on a Saturday for the annual international film festival, but we didn't have reservations for either lodgings or the films themselves. However, through the tourist bureau, we were able to find a room at a bed and breakfast that resembled a sanitarium, with postings for various treatments. My son and his girlfriend decided to camp in the rain.

Because they are vegetarians, we searched for a suitable restaurant in the *Lonely Planet* guide. Alas, it was a smoke pit, infused with the bitter aroma of European cigarettes. As far as the food, nearly everything was fried. Allen didn't know what he was eating—just that it wasn't vegetarian and may have been *Schweinhund*. I had what looked like a fried hot dog on a stick. We also took the waters. Lacking one of the porcelain cups on sale everywhere, we used our plastic water bottles, which don't produce the same effect. I had a royal allergy attack.

Sunday morning, we headed up to the film festival ticket office. Not much was available, but we managed to score tickets to a classic 1954 Hungarian film in a small movie theater at the other end of town. After climbing up a hill to get there, we sat down in the small theater only to discover that the film was indeed in Hungarian, but with subtitles in Czech. We shot glances at one another and walked out, disturbing those around us.

When we reached the box office, we needed our receipt for a refund. We reached into our bags and pockets, to no avail. Thinking we might have dropped it in the theater, we walked across town once again. My son went into the theater, disturbing everybody a second time. Fortunately, he found the receipt on the floor. Then we headed back to the ticket office and explained our plight. Apparently, we had gone to the only film that *didn't* have English subtitles.

We bought tickets to Robert Altman and Neve Campbell's *Company* in the grand ballroom of the Grandhotel Pupp, probably the fanciest down-at-the-heels hotel I've ever seen. Since we had a couple of hours before the film, we decided to take the waters at the thermal baths. Alas, the swimming pool was not very thermal—it was freezing—and Allen and I had to share towels with my son and his girlfriend, as we hadn't brought our own. As we were leaving, we discovered that towels were available for rent!

After the film, it was 7:00 p.m. and we needed to return to Prague, a four-hour-plus train ride or a two-and-a-half-hour bus ride. Unfortunately, we couldn't seem to find a timetable, so we headed to the combination bus and train depot down the hill. But no trains or buses at that station were headed for Prague. However, a Prague-bound train was leaving in eleven minutes from a station at the other end of town. We hopped into a cab, arrived at the other station, ran down the tracks, and boarded the train seconds before it pulled out. The kind conductor motioned us on, allowing us to buy our tickets on the train. I doubt the Caltrain people would have done that!

Our dinner on the train was the remnants of the apricot jam I had made from our Palo Alto tree, accompanied by the bread my son had bought that morning, the Perugina chocolate my mother had given to us between planes in New York, a shared peach, and bottled water. Later the train conductor helped us forage for food. The prepackaged boxes contained a liver paste that tasted and smelled like cat food and crackers that sounded like broken glass when we bit into them. After dinner, Allen lapsed into an Italian aria, causing the Czech rider sharing our compartment to grin, or was it grimace? We arrived at our Prague hotel shortly after midnight and sank into bed.

CHAPTER 19

SINGING IN AN ARENA, TANGLING WITH 'GENTILES' IN ISRAEL

2006

During a synagogue trip to Israel, Allen expanded his international singing chops by soloing in the old Roman amphitheater at Caesarea, north of Tel Aviv. Prodded by congregants, he sang "Eili, Eili" ("My God, My God"), based on a Hannah Senesh poem also known as "A Walk to Caesarea."

Hannah Senesh was a Zionist who left Hungary as a teen for the British Mandate of Palestine. While there, she wrote stunning poems, many of them now set to music. During World War II, she trained as a paratrooper and took a dangerous mission to occupied Hungary, where she was captured by Nazis. She was imprisoned, tortured, and ultimately executed in 1944, at age twenty-two.

"Eili, Eili" is an uplifting message about the beauty of the seascape. The translation begins with the words, "Eili, my God, I pray that these things never end. The sand and the sea, the rush of the waters, the crash of the heavens, the prayer of the heart."

As Allen stood in the amphitheater, he sang a cappella, and Israeli preteens on a school tour set aside their cell phones to listen. Then they asked him to sing it again.

"Only if you'll join in," he said, and they did.

In a High Holiday sermon later that year, Rabbi Janet Marder reflected on the synagogue trip, citing Allen's singing as the most memorable moment— not simply because Allen sang beautifully but because dozens of blasé Israeli kids, transfixed, sang with him.

Atop a mountain in the Golan Heights, I struck up a conversation with two Americans in the ladies' room line. One was a blond woman from Texas, the other a brunette from Pennsylvania. From their badges, I could tell they were not Jewish. We chatted briefly, and one woman asked me whether I was with a group.

"I'm here with my synagogue, Congregation Beth Am in Los Altos Hills, California."

"Is that a messianic congregation?" one of the women asked.

"Oh God, no!" I responded.

The women, who called themselves "messianic gentiles," were in Israel on a Zola Levitt Ministries tour. Levitt, who died in 2006, was a Jewish-born Christian and a television preacher. Messianic Judaism, which is a Protestant movement that includes Jews for Jesus, superimposes Jewish metaphors on Christian dogma. (Because Messianic Jews worship Jesus, Judaism's major denominations do not recognize it as a form of Judaism.)*

---

*   Tamar Fox, "Who Are Messianic 'Jews'?", *My Jewish Learning*, www.myjewishlearning.com/article/messianic-judaism/

"Well, the Lord bless you anyway," the Texan said as I was about to duck into a stall.

Afterward, she approached me at the sink and asked if she had said something that offended me. Then she and her friend asked me about *Yeshua*, the Hebrew name Messianic Jews use for Jesus. One of their tactics is to make the name of Jesus sound less churchy. I said that I viewed Jesus as a post-biblical prophet, adding that many of his teachings were also espoused by Rabbi Hillel, whom they had never heard of. They didn't know about the Talmud either.

While remaining calm, I told them that we Jews have no problems with Christians, or with Christianity, but we don't think it's okay for Christians to try to convert Jews. I also told them that in the eyes of mainstream Judaism, you can't be both Jewish and Christian. "We are an endangered species," I emphasized. "If you try to turn Jews into Christians, you're not our friends."

Nodding, these women thanked me profusely for teaching them about Judaism. What upsets me is that these women, who are genuinely interested in the Jewish roots of Christianity, are receiving a distorted picture. It's a shame that they don't have the opportunity to dialogue with committed Jews. On the other hand, having worked in the Jewish community, I know that not many people are willing to dialogue with Messianics. It's a dilemma.

After the synagogue trip ended, Allen and I traveled on our own to Haifa, where he lectured at the Technion, the Israel Institute of Technology.

Dan Ritter, Allen's liaison at the Technion, picked us up at our hotel and drove us around the port city, which was the first sight of Israel for so many refugees. Dan's parents came from Germany. Given that background, he is disturbed that so many Israelis these days are self-identifying as right wing, a label he considers particularly abhorrent, considering its associations with fascism.

We talked about the rifts in Israel—religious versus secular, Jew versus Arab—and he was surprised that we were going on to Safed, a northern Israel city that is the center of Jewish mysticism. Among secular Jews like Dan, Safed has a reputation for being off-the-charts odd. We soon discovered that for ourselves. Haifa, by contrast, has a reputation for being a "mixed" city, where Arabs and Jews get along. But Dan said that Arabs and Jews live in separate neighborhoods and the two cultures don't really mix.

While Allen lectured at the Technion, I went to the Coler California Visitors Center, where I received a wonderful orientation from Amir. Before playing the first of a couple of films for me, he apologized. "They're a bit sappy," he said. I soon learned that much of the information at the visitor's center is geared toward making donors feel good. Indeed, this campus is liberally festooned with plaques in English filled with the names of donors, many from Silicon Valley. In Judaism, the highest form of charity is anonymous, but you would not know it here. I'm proud to be a member of a synagogue with no donor plaques.

Nonetheless, the Technion, which graduates a sizeable percentage of Israel's engineers, has much to be proud of, including four Nobel Prize laureates, as of this writing. Face recognition software was developed here, and the topographical database that enables computer users to "travel" worldwide was also perfected here. Some of the advancements—like noninvasive imagery of the digestive tract, now used in medical operations—emerged from defense technology.

I steered Amir off-topic, and he shared his experience in the Israeli army. He said that unlike the US Army, the Israel Defense Forces is "an army of kids, not a professional army." That professionalism comes later, in the reserves, but the mandatory three years of military service are "boot camp. . . . We don't have time to train. We're like boys in a sandbox, but with much bigger toys."

We picked up our rental car and arrived in Safed (also spelled *Tzfat*) by early evening. I don't know how we managed to find our hotel, the Rimonim, but after asking directions a few times, we stumbled upon it. We wandered into the Artists' Quarter and spoke to several artists at work. One was a multimedia artist named Rely Wasser, whose work is highly symbolic. She created a Jerusalem painting made up of zippers and stones, symbolizing that Jerusalem is a city that binds us together.

The next day we pulled out our street map and began exploring the many layers of Safed, from the citadel at the top of the hill to the famed rabbis' graves at the bottom. In between are the commercial district, the Jewish Quarter, the Artists' Quarter, and the Breslav Quarter (another Jewish Quarter), where Hassidic Jews speak Yiddish, rather than Hebrew. One can climb the hill from one layer to another or board an elevator in a commercial building.

During our meanderings, we met a man known locally as "the California rebbe." He claimed to have been born in Safed and said he is the twelfth descendant of the Ba'al Shem Tov, the founder of Hassidism. Although he had a perfect American accent, he said he is a native of Israel and can't read English. He claimed he learned to speak English from his California-born wife of thirty-five years. (Later one of the gallery people told us that if it's the guy she's thinking of, he can't read English because he's dyslexic. Somebody else said he used to be a California surfer who came to Safed about a year before our visit.)

Dressed in a black hat and the garb of a Hassid along with small sunglasses, the California rebbe walked around Safed with a silver *tzedakah* (charity) box and asked for money to help poor families. Eating lunch outside in the middle of the Jewish Quarter, we wound up conversing with young English and American expatriates. Dan, from San Francisco, played the guitar and told us not to believe anything the California rebbe or anybody else in Safed says. "The first thing you have to do here is stop listening to people," he said. "People here are concerned with God's truth, not human truths."

Observing that so many of the religious folk sitting in the square were smoking, I asked the California rebbe about the compatibility of smoking and halachah (Jewish law). As I see it, the principle of preserving life from Maimonides's *Pirkei Avot* (Wisdom of the Fathers) would prohibit smoking. But many religious Israelis don't see it that way. Then the California rebbe pointed out a strikingly attractive woman at another table. "See that woman? Her name is Naomi," he said. "She's forty-six and dying of lung cancer and she can't stop smoking. . . . You can't bring the California way of thinking to Israel. It doesn't work."

Turning to another topic, I asked the California rebbe about the rabbinic prohibition against men hearing women sing. He thinks it's okay if three women sing at the same time because "then you can't tell who is singing." He also emphasized that the singing of women is seductive.

"What about Elvis?" I asked.

"Who's Elvis?" he responded. Whereupon Dan from San Francisco began riffing on "You Ain't Nothin' but a Hound Dog." Allen joined in, using his best Elvis voice, backed up by a bunch of neo-Hassidim.

Moving on, Allen and I were searching for a particular Sephardic synagogue, but it was closed. A teenage boy who had spotted us offered to guide us to a famous rabbi's grave. Before we reached the grave, we saw remnants of plastic bags and bits of cloth tied to a tree. It reminded me of the Catholic shrines of Europe, where people leave mementos, something that is decidedly un-Jewish, but as I've learned, there are many kinds of Jewish.

After showing us the grave, the young boy tried to hit us up for twenty dollars for his "poor family," what with Passover coming, etc. We gave him ten shekels ($2.25 at the time).

Later that day, we were planning to dine at Palacio, a French-Italian restaurant near the hotel. But when we arrived, the restaurant had three strikes against it. There were no diners, it was expensive, and the kid who had tried to get twenty dollars from us was standing by the bar. He was the owner's son. After looking at the menu, we said it was more than we wanted to spend, so we left.

We wound up at Hamifgash, an eclectic restaurant on the main drag, where we had the best St. Peter's fish (tilapia) we'd ever tasted. It was from the Sea of Galilee. At the next table were a bunch of young Americans who were studying at yeshivas (Orthodox seminaries) in Safed. One of them gave me a miniature religious text and asked me to carry it with me. The print is so tiny that one would have to be a Lilliputian to read it. It is still with me. So is the scratched crystal I received from an alternative healer in San Jose, California. So far, neither has changed my life.

Wrote Allen: *We're still trying to process the experience. It may take months.*

I will never be able to sing "Eili-Eili," or any other songs about Israel, without feeling a new connection between land and music, the people and myself. Sadly, our return trip to Israel in 2020 was canceled. Covid happened.

CHAPTER 20

*CONFRONTING PRIMAL FEARS IN TANZANIA**

2013

*P*laying into old stereotypes, one of my friends delights in teasing more adventurous Jews with the following litany: "Jews don't ski. Jews don't hike. Jews don't camp."

"If that were the case," I quipped, "we'd still be in Egypt."

Of course, Jews do all those things, even though some of us came from families that went berserk over skinned knees.

Chances are, that friend would have ribbed me before my safari in Tanzania, and my late parents would have issued multiple warnings, like don't drink the tap water—as if! We were in areas where there were no taps.

But ever since I read a 1995 *Jewish Bulletin* story about a Northern California

---

* An earlier version of this chapter appeared on August 2, 2013, in *J. The Jewish News of Northern California*.

woman who was mauled by a hyena in her tent in Kenya,[*] I harbored a few qualms myself. Although I had received pills for malaria and shots for typhoid, polio, yellow fever, and hepatitis A and B, there is no immunization for angst. Not only was I terrified of hyenas, but of open-mouthed crocodiles waiting for wandering wildebeests, elephants trampling Land Rovers, and lions lurking outside my tent.

Fears ran deep in my psyche. When I was a little kid, I was deathly afraid of the Big Bad Wolf, thinking he could crawl up the fire escape into my bedroom window, and if a friend played his *Peter and the Wolf* record, I would run out of the room before the wolf devoured the duck.

But as a journalist, I have confronted my fears. I traveled to Israel during the height of the second intifada, scaled a cliff for an assignment on rock climbing, and even witnessed a cremation. In that spirit, when my husband and three of his Peace Corps buddies from the 1960s decided to return to Tanzania in 2013, I agreed to join them. After all, the Ba'al Shem Tov, the founder of Hassidism, commanded us to get out into nature and be joyful, and this was a golden opportunity. Besides, to kvetch may be human, but it is hardly divine.

Our group of seven debarked at Kilimanjaro International Airport, shelled out two crisp fifty dollar bills each for visas, and checked into a tropical lodge, where we dined on tasty chicken in coconut sauce.

Was this a reassuring prelude to ominous encounters of the mammalian kind? Would a crazed bull elephant in musth (testosterone overload) later cross our path? Would lions and hyenas prowl outside our tent at night, eager to get their paws on my stash of chocolate, or worse?

The next morning, Douglas, our guide, said we would focus not just on wildlife and scenery, but on Tanzania's diverse cultures and its concerns. Our first stop was Light in Africa, where we hugged small children whose parents had succumbed to AIDS.

---

[*] Teresa Strasser, "Kenyas Jews rally for Marin woman after hyena attack," *J. The Jewish News of Nothern California* (August 25, 1995), https://jweekly.com/1995/08/25/kenya-s-jews-rally-for-marin-woman-after-hyena-attack/

As our journey continued, we went on a bush walk with Watuni and Kiaro, Maasai warriors who carried spears and cell phones, and their buddy Toroye, a former hunter-gatherer. We walked in silence and were told to freeze if Douglas held his hand up, indicating danger.

The dangers lay elsewhere: raging Homo sapiens. Not far from our camp, a United Arab Emirates–based corporation had built a lodge and a private airstrip so sheikhs and their invited guests could fly in to shoot lions with rifles because they have purchased that right from the Tanzanian government.

Over the course of fifteen days, my irrational fears slowly dissipated. On my last night in Tanzania, I heard a lioness outside our tent and then a howling hyena. Smiling, I rolled over and went back to sleep.

But serious concerns now threaten to keep me awake: trophy seekers, not to mention trappers who sell these animals to zoos and circuses. That said, I was proud of another thing that Jews, by tradition, don't do: Jews don't hunt for sport.

In the remote Loliondo Game Controlled Area where few tourists venture, we were a curiosity. As we entered the Maasai compound, children rushed to meet us, inspecting our cameras, our clothing, and the pictures on an iPad. A toddler who wore no pants piggybacked on his curious older sister. Many of the children had flies on their eyes and lips, which didn't seem to bother them.

Elizabeth, the first of three wives of a Maasai herder, had little acquaintance with modern technology. But she had a cell phone, enabling her to keep in touch with her husband, who was off herding cattle, accompanied by his third wife.

Eleven children lived in that *enkang* (Maasai enclosure), which featured a fence at the perimeter to enclose the sheep, goats, and cattle; a field for corn;

and three *bomas* (round mud huts), one for each of the three wives. Five of the children belonged to Elizabeth, who wore large silver earrings and cloths of several patterns draped on her body. One of these cloths formed a sling for baby Michaela, whom she carried on her back.

She invited us into her boma, which she had built herself. She had gathered the wood to support the structure and plastered the walls with fresh cow dung, which hardened in the heat.

Despite a fire on the floor, the boma was dark, and we could neither understand Elizabeth's words nor read her expressions. Elizabeth, who lives on a Maasai enkang in northern Tanzania, speaks only the Maasai language. A tribesman translated her words into Swahili. Douglas, our guide, retranslated into English.

"Do you have cows?" Elizabeth asked as we sat on the floor of her boma.

We seven Americans—four 1960s Peace Corps veterans and three family members—were retired engineers and teachers, a building contractor, and a journalist. We lived in cities and suburbs, not on farms, and we had no cows.

Because cows are the measure of wealth among the Maasai, Elizabeth was baffled: "If you don't have cows, how do you get milk?" she asked. Milk and cornmeal are the mainstays of her diet. In the enkang, as in most of Tanzania, there is no refrigeration, no electricity, no farm machinery, no running water. Without access to a cow, there is no milk.

To Americans and Europeans traveling in northern Tanzania and Kenya, the Maasai have become a tourist attraction, and safari lodges hire them to transport luggage and protect guests from beasts who stray too close to tent-cabins. With their distinctive red cloaks, tall spears, and elaborate earrings and jewelry, the Maasai cut striking figures—particularly as they now carry cell phones along with their spears, using solar chargers.

Polygamy didn't seem to pose a problem to Elizabeth. In the Maasai culture, marriages are economic contracts between families and are arranged. While her husband was away, Elizabeth slept in the boma with her children and the animals. But when her husband returns and wants to sleep with her, the children and, presumably, the animals will be sent to the boma of another wife.

However, as Maasai convert to Christianity and women become more educated, polygamy may be declining. Among the six Maasai men working at our campsite, only one had two wives. Some of the younger men said one wife was enough.

Another practice that is declining is female circumcision, which is now illegal in Tanzania and neighboring Kenya. Traditionally, to be considered marriageable, Maasai girls were forced to undergo the rite at puberty. Teachers and community health workers are encouraging a substitute rite of passage that does not include cutting. However, female circumcision is still practiced clandestinely, often among girls well below the age of puberty, our guide reported.

When we returned to our campsite, I couldn't help noticing a goat tethered to a tree. "Is that goat a pet or is it dinner?" I said half-jokingly to Hagai, a Maasai tribesman who worked for our tour company.

"Dinner," he said with a smile.

Stifling my squeamish stomach, I documented the killing with my camera, from the strangling of the goat to the sucking of its blood to the butchering. *If I'm going to eat meat*, I said to myself, *I should know where it comes from*. I am still an omnivore, and was able to dine on the roasted goat, but I have never been able to look at the pictures of the killing.

As we sat around the campfire after dinner, the Maasai entertained us with a chant and a dance, traditionally performed after the killing of a lion. Although the Maasai are pastoralists, not hunter-gatherers, the killing of a lion remains a rite of passage, and several tribesmen boasted about how many lions they had killed. The camp cook, who is Maasai but lives in a city and wears Western clothes, has neither killed nor cooked a lion. He laughed at the prospect. Maasai don't eat game.

Our guide found it ironic that a billionaire from the United Arab Emirates is entitled to hunt on the land with rifles, while local tribesmen are forbidden to hunt with bows and arrows or graze their cattle on land where they have traditionally lived. Their presence threatens the livelihood of the Maasai. That's why they have mobilized politically to protect their lands. But in 2022, "dozens of police personnel arrived to reportedly evict Maasai tribespeople in the (Loliondo) area in order to make way for a game reserve for the United Arab Emirates (UAE) royal family," according to Survival International and the Oakland Institute.*

During our 2013 visit, the situation was less calamitous, enabling us to trade information about our lives with the tribespeople. We broached the subject of marriage and divorce.

"If a couple wants to divorce, do the families have to give permission?" we were asked. In Tanzania, the families must approve.

"Who gets the children?" we wondered.

In Tanzania, it is the husband. If a woman leaves her husband and takes the children with her, her own parents may force her to return the children to the husband.

Since Allen had been divorced, he was asked if he needed his first wife's approval before he could marry me.

The Americans laughed at the notion.

"Polygamy is illegal," I explained. "But if an American no longer loves his first wife, he can divorce her and remarry. If he tires of the second wife, he can divorce her and remarry, and so on. But we can't have two wives or two husbands at the same time."

In Tanzania, divorce is legal but difficult because marriage is a contract that involves both families. Since divorce is rare, we wanted to know what would happen if a Maasai man no longer loved his wife and wasn't in a position to

---

* Rajat Ghai, "Fortress Conservation: Tension in Tanzania's Loliondo as troops move in to evict Maasai to make way for game reserve," *DowntoEarth* (June 10, 2022), https://www.downtoearth.org.in/news/africa/fortress-conservation-tension-in-tanzania-s-loliondo-as-troops-move-in-to-evict-maasai-to-make-way-for-game-reserve-83248

take a second wife.

The Maasai shook their heads. One said such a scenario was inconceivable, as they are required to love their wives.

But then Arthur, one of the Peace Corps veterans, pointed out that wives like Elizabeth build the huts, cook the meals, milk the cows, care for the children, and tend the crops.

"The women do all the work," he said. "Why *should* you divorce them?"

At that the Maasai laughed.

CHAPTER 21

A POST-CUBA PASSOVER

2015

*T*he downside of travel is what's euphemistically called *turista*. It hit me on our last day in Tanzania, and it struck again two days after we returned from Cuba, just before Passover.

Why now? I thought. *I was fine in Cuba. Was it something I ate in the airport?* When the digestive symptoms ebbed, I came down with a full-blown respiratory infection. So did my husband. We spent the week housebound.

By Tuesday evening, I could not put dinner on the table. When my busy stepdaughter, Shani, phoned that evening, I begged her to send over chicken soup. Thank you, Shani.

By Wednesday, I realized I was in no position to host the seders planned for Friday and Saturday. I couldn't cook, clean, or even get off the sofa, where my husband and I camped at either end. I sent out APBs to family members invited for Friday and to friends who were coming on Saturday.

"We are sorry to pass over Passover this year, but we are two droopy *Snuf-fleupaguses* and can't see clear to a celebration," I wrote.

Feeling somewhat better on Friday, I ran out to buy a brisket, at which point it dawned on me that the five-pound slab of meat cost what the average Cuban earns in a couple of months. But I was determined to at least capture some of the holiday's spirit. I clipped azalea blooms from our garden and put them in a bud vase on the dining room table, set two places, filled a pewter cup with Concord grape wine, and lit the candles. Then my stepdaughter brought over two plastic containers filled with matzah ball soup. A blessing.

We had prepared no seder plate, no kugel, no tzimmes (sweet carrot and prune casserole), and no sponge cake. We didn't even open the Haggadah. But as we sat down to dinner, grateful for our abundance, we counted our blessings. That Passover was our Thanksgiving. It wasn't about cooking, cleaning, shopping, or the busyness that plagues me when I host. Instead, it was an opportunity to take a deep breath and utter thanks.

That others aren't so fortunate was driven home to me during a visit to a professional family in their Havana apartment, well off the government-sponsored tourist circuit. We had been invited by a Cuban colleague of a Silicon Valley friend and were told to bring another couple along. We had thought it was a dinner invitation.

When we arrived, laden with small gifts, our host told us that the taxi driver who brought us earns more in a couple of hours than he and his wife earn in a month. The discrepancies between those who benefit from the tourist economy and those who receive government salaries—about twenty dollars a month at the time—were staggering.

At 7:00 p.m., we sat down at the family's kitchen table, chatting about education, the Bay of Pigs, Cuban history. The couple, both fluent in English, wanted their daughter to practice her conversation. We sang "Old MacDonald," accompanied by my husband's boisterous animal noises.

Our host's kitchen—they had no living room—contained a refrigerator, a double burner on the countertop, no oven, and no microwave. We saw no signs of food preparation, and nothing was offered. Suddenly we realized there had been some miscommunication. With food severely rationed, the Cubans couldn't possibly afford to feed four extra mouths.

At 9:00 p.m., we invited the family out for dinner. They graciously accepted, bringing us to a private Cuban restaurant frequented by tourists. The American educators at the next table let us ride back to the city center in their tour bus, saving us another cab fare. Despite our misunderstanding, the evening was a joyous one, which we ended in a jazz club.

We thought about the Cuban experience on Passover, when we open our doors, inviting all who are hungry to come in and eat. We need to do a better job at recognizing the very real hunger in our midst and doing what we can do to allay it. The various international and local hunger projects need our contributions, not just at holiday time.

Being ill and hungry during a holiday brought home a more personal lesson: Because of misplaced pride, I had trouble admitting that I needed help. When I bring meals to friends and synagogue families who are coping with illness or hardship, I tell them that asking for help when they need it is as much of a mitzvah as delivering it.

Yet with the tables turned, I had trouble asking. I won't make that mistake again.

CHAPTER 22

WHO NEEDS SATURDAY? A LONG NIGHT'S JOURNEY INTO A HONG KONG DAY

2018

Nothing is permanent, the Buddhists point out, so I try to relish the unexpected, which is why we travel. What was also impermanent was the peaceful Hong Kong we experienced in 2018, before Beijing's crackdowns and human rights violations changed the tenor of the city.

Our journey began with an airport check-in on a Friday night and a Sunday morning arrival in Hong Kong fifteen hours later, when we set our watches sixteen hours ahead. I slept through an abbreviated Saturday, drifting off during takeoff and skipping Cathay Pacific's 2:00 a.m. dinner tray.

Who needs Saturday, anyway? A leisurely Sunday is a good start. We picked up our bags and spotted a man carrying a placard with our misspelled surname. Thanks to Overseas Adventure Travel, a limousine escorted us to our hotel. Along the way, we passed magnificent seascapes and islands surrounded by mountains.

After unpacking, we left the hotel and found a modest restaurant around the corner. The menu featured such soups as figs, jelly fungus, and sea coconut or dried duck stomach, sweet date, and white cabbage. We opted for the familiar wonton soup, dumplings, and tea. Unfortunately, we had no Hong Kong money, and the restaurant wouldn't accept credit cards. The kindly manager sent me next door to the ATM at the 7-Eleven, but the ATM rejected my debit card. Would we have to wash dishes? Fortunately, my husband had it all worked out. In the restaurant, a Canadian expatriate from Calgary overheard our dilemma and exchanged one hundred dollars in US money for Hong Kong dollars, at the going rate. It was a win-win: He needed stable currency. We needed usable dollars. We shook hands and set off to tour the town.

Before the trip, we had purchased Hong Kong travel passes, which included twenty-four hours on a hop-on, hop-off Big Red Bus. But we couldn't find a bus stop. Wearing our most quizzical looks, we were greeted by a young couple who asked, "Can we help you?" They escorted us on a fifteen-minute trek past myriad high-end shops such as Tiffany, Louis Vuitton, and Michael Kors. The main island of Hong Kong, we discovered, was a massive upscale shopping mall interspersed with side streets where street vendors plied finger bananas, fruits we'd never seen before, and fresh fish.

After finding a Big Red Bus stop, we hopped on. Not exactly sure where to go, we opted for the botanical-zoological garden, a small woodsy zoo on Victoria Peak. We sat on a bench and watched flamingos on a pond behind us and a bird with a reddish Woody Woodpecker mop in a garden patch in front of us. The children, too, were colorfully clad in Sunday play clothes, wearing sunhats and novelty sneakers, while their chic moms, in stylish sundresses or cropped pants and tunics, looked like they were ready for the runway. This was obviously a moneyed town, albeit with pockets of poverty. As we walked out of the gardens and down the hill, we passed Teslas, BMWs, Mercedes, and an occasional Prius like ours. Nissans? Hyundais? Kias? Chevys? Forget it.

However, one bizarre Sunday sight stopped us cold: Near the train station, groups of women sat on flattened cardboard boxes on the sidewalks, which they covered with plastic tablecloths. Cell phones in hand and lunches in foil or plastic containers, they ate, played cards, and gossiped. The younger women, who didn't seem to carry an array of edibles, sat together on ledges in the shade of office buildings, checking their phones, sipping takeout coffee, and occasionally talking to each other.

Why were they on the sidewalks and ledges? They are Hong Kong's domestic workers, mostly from the Philippines and Indonesia, I found out later. Sundays are traditionally a day off for live-in maids. Since the women don't have homes suitable for socializing, and restaurants are beyond their budget, they often choose a spot on the street for their weekly gatherings. Some choose one of Hong Kong's many parks, but on the Sunday when we visited, the nearby Chater Garden had been taken over by the Jewish community for the city's thirty-third annual Hanukkah festival and candle lighting. Sponsored by the Orthodox Chabad as well as Hong Kong's largely expatriate Jewish community, the festival drew mostly American and Israeli residents plus a smattering of Asians and tourists like us.

The children at the festival, more casually dressed than the Asians at the zoological garden, enjoyed arts and crafts, games, and noshes. Some took turns churning latke batter with a food processor attached to the back of a bicycle; as the kids pedal, the processor blades churn the batter. As our long day ended, the latkes and the sound of Israeli and American voices brought the spirit of the holiday home to us. My self-described atheist husband considered joining the all-male minchah (evening prayer) service, because it would be an experience, but instead he ate another latke. A higher calling, he said.

By that point, we had walked for miles and had no idea how to return to our hotel at the other end of the city. An Israeli advised against walking and directed us to an underground station across the street. Finding our way in was easy. We just followed the crowd. Finding our way out at Hong Kong's

Time Square Station was another challenge. We took escalators up and escalators down, passing myriad shops with English and European names and an upscale food court—no Panda Express here—but we couldn't find a pathway out of the underground to the street. Were we doomed to wander for hours in a shopping center, my husband's definition of hell? But since English was spoken here, we asked a fashionably dressed concierge for directions to the outside.

Too tired for dinner at a restaurant, we stumbled upon a take-out dim sum place where Hong Kong residents lined up. Nearby, a fruit stall offered finger bananas and mandarin oranges. Eventually, we found our hotel. We entered the room, flung our shoes to the floor, wolfed down our makeshift supper, and collapsed. Thirty-one hours after we left home, we fell into bed at 8:00 p.m. Hong Kong time, 4:00 a.m. in California. It had been a long day without a Saturday. Our compensation: a forty-hour sleepless Wednesday on the way home from Bangkok.

CHAPTER 23

THAILAND: LADYBOYS, TRANS BARS, AND CABBAGES & CONDOMS

2018

Thailand is hot, humid, and oppressive, even in December, but in the Land of Smiles, the warmth of the people is overwhelming. We learned to bow every time we greeted someone, using the words *sawadee kha* (men say *sawadee khrap*). After a while, it became second nature. I had more difficulty with the words for "thank you" (*khop koon kha*) and got the syllables confused. Maybe it was the heat.

Wan, our guide, explained Thai etiquette: smile, bow, and never raise your voice, act angry, or make disparaging remarks about the royal family. Then she began to tell us about herself, illuminating more of her story as the days progressed and we traveled through the streets of Thailand's cities and villages. In the villages, we watched elders cobble together a living by weaving baskets, farming, keeping traditional crafts alive, and entertaining curious tourists through organizations such as Overseas Adventure Travel. But the young people leave home for better opportunities. Some go to a university. Some become monks. Some head for the cities, to work in factories, restaurants, hotels, and bars.

Wan's own backstory is not atypical. She had left a rural community in Chiang Mai province and went to Malaysia, finding work in a factory. At some point, she married, gave birth to two sons, divorced, and became a tour guide. After becoming a single mother, her family life took a different direction. "I had two sons. Now I have a son and a daughter," she said matter-of-factly. One son was a novice at the time, training to be a Buddhist monk. After undergoing gender reassignment surgery, her other child, a university graduate, became a woman. Thailand is the leading world center for gender-reassignment surgery, where it is a multibillion-dollar industry. Since 1975, Thai doctors have been doing gender-reassignment surgery, primarily male to female.[*]

Detouring from our tour package, one evening Wan invited us to accompany her to a Bangkok trans bar, where a couple dozen attractive "ladyboys" (*kathoey* in Thai), dressed in red and black bikinis, gyrated to music. One stepped off the stage and sat next to a man on our right. I didn't want to stare, but Allen caught a glimpse: "Lap sex," he said.

Most of the performers had undergone at least one surgery: breast implants. Meena, a friend of Wan's who sat with us, had undergone several surgeries. She came from a rural area in north Thailand and headed to Bangkok, according to Wan. At one point, she was involved with a Japanese man who paid for her breast implants. Later, she was involved with another Japanese man who paid for genital surgery. Another common procedure is removal of the telltale Adam's apple, plus the facial surgery to remove traces of facial hair.

It was too noisy in the bar for me to have much of a conversation with Meena, and photos were prohibited, but I did pose one question: Did she prefer men or women?

"Men," she said, vociferously. Then she lifted her bikini top, revealing her

---

[*]   "The Development of Sex Reassignment Surgery in Thailand: A Social Perspective," *Scientific World Journal*, 2014.

small, firm breasts and asked if we wanted to feel them. I declined, but Allen copped a squeeze. I did smooth her straight silken hair, which could have been featured in a shampoo ad. It was not a wig.

In the bar, the trans women are considered employees, compensated by the establishment. If a man invites one to sit down next to him, he pays for her drink and his own. That's how the bar makes money. If they leave the bar together, that is a negotiation, and the patron pays a "fine" to the bar for taking the ladyboy out of service.

The sex trade, which first blossomed to serve American soldiers during the Vietnam War, is now a multibillion-dollar business. As we rode on a wild *tuk-tuk* ride through Bangkok's Chinatown, we passed dozens of gorgeously costumed women. Bangkok's Red Light District is replete with sex entertainment venues, brothels, and bars. These venues are legal, yet prostitution has been illegal since 1960.

"The police are paid off," Wan said.

Thailand Development Research Institute estimated that Thailand's sex trade is a $6.4 billion business, accounting for about 10 to 12 percent of the country's gross domestic product in 2015.[*] Thailand's sex workers number at least 250,000 in a country of 70 million. Before Thailand restricted international travel amid the coronavirus, sex workers sent an average of $300 million a year to family members in the country's rural areas.[†]

We learned that attractive but not well-educated Thai teens are recruited from the poorer northern provinces, often by other women who have been in the sex trade. These recruiters approach the families, promising that their daughters can make a good living in Bangkok. Some of the families, led to believe their daughters are working in hotels or restaurants, may have no idea

[*]   *TDRI Insight*, July 21, 2022. Amid the coronavirus, Thailand has restricted international travel, which has crippled the sex trade economy, according to a 2021 *NPR* article. The GDP in Thailand in 2015 was about $401 billion.

[†]   Havocscope is an international database that compiles information on the global black market.

of the nature of the business. Some may know but pretend not to. Regardless, with the money sent home, the families can buy bigger and better homes, and the young women feel they're doing good by supporting their families. Eventually, these women may return to their hometowns. Or they may marry foreign men. Apparently, Japanese men are supposed to be good husbands, particularly favored by transgender women, according to Wan.

Toward the end of the trip, Wan took us to a roadside restaurant called C&C, shorthand for Cabbages & Condoms. Along with utensils, a colorfully wrapped condom sat at every place setting, and at the entrance was a stylized condom with a sign, "Our food is guaranteed not to cause pregnancy." The adjoining shop also sold contraceptive-themed T-shirts and other souvenirs. Despite its catchy name and condom jokes, C&C calls itself a serious "business for social progress," supporting not only family planning and HIV/AIDS education, but community health, rural development, and environmental concerns.

For Wan herself, who comes from the rural north, that AIDS education mission is personal. Two of her siblings died of AIDS, both from heterosexual encounters during the epidemic in the 1980s. Her sister contracted AIDS through her husband. For her brother, the infection resulted from a rite of passage. His friend took him to a prostitute following his graduation from high school. Both the friend and the brother contracted AIDS, her brother becoming blind before he succumbed. The friend also died. A third sibling died shortly after birth, and after the death of her father, Wan and her mother are the sole survivors.

Wan's family is considerably smaller now, and biological grandchildren are not on the horizon, with one child a monk and the other a trans woman. Acceptance of the transition was particularly difficult for Wan's mother. But Wan focused in on the importance of family.

"Do you love your granddaughter?" she asked her mother.

Wan's mother hesitated, but she nodded and said yes. Thailand is a Land of Smiles.

CHAPTER 24

THE FRENCH CONNECTION

2001–Present

On a Friday evening in southwest France, Palo Alto's Aurora Singers brought a cowboy medley and a Western dance number into Albi's imposing Romanesque cathedral, much to the delight of a sell-out crowd of 850. In a 2007 concert, the group was certainly the first to perform a wacky arrangement of Lewis Carroll's "Jabberwocky," not only orchestrated with toy instruments but punctuated by frightening screams.

As we sang songs of our two nations in concert with our French compatriots from Albi's Chorale Assou Lezert, our voices melded into something greater, symbolizing the relationship between sister-city chorales that began just weeks after September 11, 2001. Through six choral exchanges over two decades, we have sustained that relationship, and when travel was out of the question, we have nurtured those ties via emails, Facebook, and Zoom. Now the Albigeois are family.

In October 2001, the Chorale Assou Lezert arrived in Palo Alto for the first time. In addition to experiencing the joy of singing together in harmony, we welcomed the visitors into our homes, sharing meals, outings, and social activities. With America and the world still reeling after the attacks, we also shared our grief. That year, the French group donated their share of the concert proceeds to the American Red Cross, aiding the victims and rescuers of the tragedy in New York.

After the concert in a Palo Alto church, the two choirs converged on our house for a last-minute cast party with close to a hundred in attendance. It was so crowded that to get from one end of the living room to the other, I had to exit the house through the back door and reenter through the front. When I asked the woman who delivered the pizzas why she was still in the house, she said she was trapped and couldn't find a way to get out. Fortunately, Allen's booming voice cleared an exit path.

Our guests discovered that we California Americans—who arrived from the East, Midwest, Europe, and Asia—are a multicultural bunch. As if to prove that premise, one friend served an Indian meal to his guests while I entertained our visitors with a typical Jewish Shabbat meal. When they spotted homemade chicken soup laden with wobbly hunks of what they perceived as a very strange *légume* (vegetable), they wondered, "*Qu'est-ce que c'est, chou-fleur?*"

No, it was not cauliflower, I said, bringing out the matzah meal box to explain what my French could not. They eyed the soup with suspicion, but they gobbled it up. Then they asked for seconds on the brisket.

After the meal, we talked about the concept of Shabbat. Séverine, a second soprano and a beautician, said she knew something about our Friday night meal. She described a comic French film about a down-and-out man on the streets of Paris's garment district who was mistaken for Jewish by Tunisian Jews. Suddenly given a job and invited to a Sephardic Shabbat dinner, where he has no idea what's going on, his friends tell him to say he's Ashkenazi. Coincidentally, we had also seen that film (*La vérité si je mens* or *Would I Lie to You?*) at San Francisco's Jewish Film Festival, and we informed our guests that we, too, are Ashkenazi, bringing smiles to the table.

These exchange visits help dispel national stereotypes. On our return visit to Albi, Séverine's father, who owns a cattle farm, asked us whether we lived on a diet of McDonald's and fast food.

"*Pas chez Allen et Janet*," Séverine informed him, describing our visit to the farmers' market, which culminated in an al fresco lunch of gazpacho, sourdough bread, and salads.

Not all Americans relish fast food, and not all French are fabled cooks, nor do they prepare everything themselves. In fact, when baritone Laurent served us a magnificent-looking paella, which we praised to the hilt, he blushingly admitted that it came from the restaurant next door. The equally magnificent-looking tiramisu, however, he proudly proclaimed was his own.

Over the years, we have borrowed one another's traditions. Some of the American singers now include a cheese course at the end of their dinner parties. Meanwhile, during a return visit to Albi, we observed that our French friends had adopted the American custom of potlucks and shared meals. Before the exchange visits, they would not have dreamed of bringing anything more than wine or chocolates to a friend's dinner party. Now they might bring a first course or a dessert. During visits to our home, our French guests now pitch in like members of the family, helping in the kitchen, jumping up to clear the table after meals, and assisting with the laundry, just as we helped our hostess in France hang the wash on her clothesline.

But quite apart from sharing food, chores, and traditions, we have shared lives, sending wedding and baby gifts and messages of condolence. We also take care of one another. When Nadine's daughter, Marion, was about to attend Dublin City University, Carole, the Irish-born widow of our late president, arranged for Marion to stay with her mother until she found housing.

On our last visit to Albi in 2017, we stayed with Nadine and Bruno, who had hosted us in 2007. On Bastille Day, which began with river rafting on the Tarn and ended with fireworks, Bruno refused to let us pay our share of an expensive restaurant dinner. He was adamant. So was Nadine when I awoke the next day with a fever and laryngitis. "I am your mother," she said. "I am taking you to my doctor. I will not take no for an answer. You are going."

Nadine, who became my Jewish mother for a day, led me to her physician and then to the pharmacy, putting everything on her own account. I could do nothing to dissuade her. However, when we stopped at a supermarket, where I picked up a few treats, I insisted on paying. Nadine smiled. "It's okay," she said. "Bruno isn't here."

I never recovered my voice in time to sing in subsequent concerts, but fortunately, I was able to join the chorales on a two-day bus trip to Lourdes and the Pyrenees. We also enjoyed dinner at the homes of those we had hosted in Palo Alto: no paella or tiramisu this time at Laurent's home. His new wife, Christine, took over the kitchen and roasted a chicken. Séverine, now married and the mother of two daughters, hosted a multicourse meal, ending with myriad desserts, some contributed by her guests. Noticing that one of Séverine's daughters had decorated her room with New York City wallpaper and bedding, I sent her a Big Apple snow globe.

Our world has grown. During their 2005 visit to California, we accompanied our French guests to Yosemite, bringing along Tim, our grandson, who was ten. He was struck by the grandeur of the national park, but even more, he enjoyed socializing with Thibault, the son of Nadine and Bruno. As Tim waved to his new friends as the buses left to take our visitors to the airport, he cried. We, too, cry as we board buses to the Toulouse airport or as we dispatch our guests to the San Francisco airport.

Amid Covid, we sent emails and postcards, and we met on Zoom to chat and rehearse. We also created virtual choral recordings, each of us singing at home into our phones or recording devices. As I write, we don't yet have the technology to sing and record together in real time, as Zoom would create a cacophony instead of a chorus. But after each individual records the songs, our techno-whiz blends the voices into choral pieces that keep our harmonies alive and preserve the memories of concerts past.

PART III

'SUNRISE, SUNSET'

CHAPTER 25

'WE'RE HERE FOR JUST A VISIT'

1999–2019

During a 2005 performance with the French choir at Stanford's Memorial Church, Allen mounted the high pulpit and bellowed his solo in "Ride the Chariot" with the spirit of a revival preacher:

"Are you ready, my brother?

"Are you ready for the journey?

"Do you want to see your Jesus?

"I'm waiting for the chariot and I'm ready to go."

He may have been too convincing. As he was leaving the church after the concert, two men approached him:

"That was you!" one of the men said. "And you were looking right at me!"

"Well, maybe I was," Allen said, playing along.

"But my friend here says you're Jewish. Are you?"

"Yes, I am."

"Whew, what a relief!"

Since we're Jewish, we have no plans to meet Jesus at the end of our journey. Regardless, we are not ready to go. However, our parents have boarded, leaving us in the waiting room. We hope we will go out loving and laughing, as my father did. But the journey is scary. When I was a child, my grandmother, her nearest sister, and her sister-in-law were widowed. "We're here for just a visit," my grandmother said. Later, my mother and the women in her building became a "mostly girls" bridge group and luncheon set. Now my girlfriends and my classmates are becoming widowed, one by one. Sometimes it's expected. Sometimes it's a shock.

While we were on a cruise in the Baltic, I opened my email to discover that a man in our social group had died. Most of us didn't know he was seriously ill. We were at sea during the funeral, but we managed to attend the last shiva (Jewish mourning gathering) the day we returned. We can't help but wonder which of us will be next. Yes, intellectually, we know that's the way things are. We pass. I'm not worried about my own passing, but the inevitable passing of those around me is nonetheless troubling.

Allen and I began our journey with two grandchildren between us, one married child, and three living parents. Now we have eight grandchildren, three married children, and one who is divorced. Our parents are gone. "Sunrise, Sunset."

Like my husband, my father loved to sing, and he would use a song—sometimes of his own invention—to keep events from becoming too heavy. He'd also chime in with his own words when somebody else broke into song. When my grandmother sang "I Wonder Who's Kissing Her Now," he'd inevitably ask, "What's her now?"

He also knew how to choose the right words to ease a sorrowful situation. That's what he did when he phoned to wish me a happy new year after the High Holidays in 1999. In a reassuring voice, he told me that his prostate cancer had returned. He had about a year. Maybe eighteen months.

"I'll be fine," he said. "They've found a new experimental medicine and the doctor is quite enthusiastic. It's not a cure, but it will improve my quality of life. Don't worry. We will be at your wedding. I wouldn't miss it for anything."

Then he added, "I've had a good life."

I held my tears until I hung up the phone. I talked to my brother. Then I called Allen. My father would indeed be at the wedding. How much longer he would live was anybody's guess.

Dad made it to our February 2000 wedding. Pearl, Allen's mother, did not. The previous Passover, she was carried on a chair to the seder by Allen and his brother. She was grateful for the opportunity to meet my parents, however briefly, during that Passover gathering at a friend's pool house. When Pearl found out we were getting married, she blessed us. She was especially happy that Allen was remarrying. To a Jewish girl, no less.

Pearl, who survived four husbands and lived until age ninety-three, could have had a fifth husband. When she was in her eighties, a man in his seventies proposed to her. She turned him down.

Her response: "Why would I want to take care of an old man?"

I first met Pearl in the spring of 1999, after a series of strokes that had landed her in a Palo Alto board-and-care home. After our visit, Allen cried on the way to the car, telling me I should have known Pearl in her earlier days.

We stopped in to see her in October 1999 before we took off for Barcelona, where Allen was about to teach a one-week course. I had arrived at Pearl's residence shortly before Allen, and Pearl was unhappy that the only woman she could converse with had moved out. As I wheeled her around the patio, Pearl looked at me and said, "You're trying to butter me up!" Then she added, "That it should come to this!" I believe the loss of her dignity was far more painful than any of the physical disabilities she endured.

While we were in Barcelona, Pearl developed pneumonia, was hospitalized, and later placed in a skilled nursing facility. When we returned from Spain, we knew she would be leaving us. We sang the Jewish lullabies her own mother had sung to her. I told her my father was thrilled to have a son-in-law he adored.

She smiled. The Monday before Thanksgiving, she slipped away. The following Friday, we held a short memorial service. Sadly, Pearl's friends weren't there. At ninety-three, she didn't have many left.

Our February 2000 wedding had a bittersweet quality because my father was clearly not well, although he danced with my mother and tried his best to celebrate. By the spring of 2001, the cancer had metastasized to his brain, and his care had become too much for my mother. One morning, he went into hospice care at Calvary Hospital so his electrolytes could be balanced. He stayed there until he died, just two months before 9/11. Allen and I sang to him, on the phone and during our visits.

To my father, whose lifelong career was in publishing, I owe my love of books and my career as a writer-editor. One skill I did not pick up was his ability to turn almost anything into a joke, including death and dying. While he was in Calvary, he would try to get a laugh by imitating a patient going through the last agonies, rolling his eyes back.

Dad, a proud secular Jew who never had a bar mitzvah and had no use for religion, was nonetheless proud of my midlife bat mitzvah in 1998. Yet one Shabbat when I recited the blessing over the candles, he looked at my daughter and said, "I want you to know, your mother didn't learn any of this from us." His favorite expression: "I hate ritual." That said, he inadvertently launched a family ritual for our Passover seders. In the 1990s, when I was leading a family seder, Dad refused to return to the table after the meal so we could complete the rituals. Instead, he sank into an armchair in the living room and repeated his favorite nonsensical blessing: My best stab: *Ashmitah haSecha, mita pupitza lecha, v'kairov tuchus, ha krechtsin zaften*. When I repeated it to my own rabbi, she said, "Well, I recognize one word." *Tuchus*, Americanized as "tushy."

When my son went to open the door for Elijah, he spotted a pink mop top in the broom closet and plunked it on my father's head. That got a rise out of Dad, who came to the table as the biblical prophet. These days, Allen plays Elijah at our family and interfaith seders, wearing a bathrobe and an old rag mop top as a head covering.

In keeping with Dad's distaste for ritual, he was not happy when Rabbi Goldman, a friend of my brother's, came to visit him at Calvary. The rabbi, as was his tradition, uttered a blessing. My father, as was his tradition, followed with *Ashmitah haSecha*, and family members tried to repress their giggles.

Nonetheless, Rabbi Goldman was in the congregation at Dad's funeral, where I opened my eulogy with the infamous *Ashmitah*. Rabbi Goldman remembered it, chuckled, and took it in good spirit. Later at the house, he said, "I gave him my blessing, he gave me his blessing."

My mother also had a sense of humor, even to the end: my father's and her own. A day or two before my father died, she asked me to make brownies. I looked at her and delivered the punchline to a favorite joke about a dying husband who smells the goodies emanating from the kitchen and asks his wife for a bite.

"That's for after," I told her.

She laughed, and we waited.

Later, when she was facing the end herself and was in a rehab-hospital facility on Long Island, she asked to be moved to Calvary, as she was impressed with the care my father had received. She was told she wasn't eligible because she didn't have cancer.

"Okay," she asked with a straight face, "how do you get cancer?"

I was with Mother for three weeks at the end of 2005, returning home to California for two weeks. Then I returned to New York for five weeks until the end. What kept me going was my emails to friends and family. Mother spent her last weeks in her own apartment. Una, a live-in hospice aide from Jamaica, stayed in the apartment until the end. So did I.

I sent the following email from New York on February 11, 2006, two weeks before Mother passed:

We are still waiting, but the visiting nurse tells us it can't be too much longer, as it's hard to survive on ice chips and tiny spoonsful of sherbet. Mother has been on what I call the North Pole diet for several weeks now—although in past days she occasionally ate a third of a scrambled egg or half a slice of toast. No longer.

Waiting is extremely difficult, and exhausting. Plus, since Mother's at home, there's work to be done, including administering morphine and helping the aide with turning and repositioning. Fortunately, we rented a great hospital bed. Before Mom came home, Allen and my son reconfigured the bedroom.

We have a wonderful aide from Jamaica, who cooked curried chicken for us tonight. What a treat. It was nice to enjoy someone else's cooking. And last night one of the neighbors, my mother's friend, made us a pot of soup. While Mother was in the hospital, we got home late and ate mostly Chinese takeout, but now we're preparing our own meals.

Cooking in someone else's kitchen is always difficult, and grocery shopping on the streets of Forest Hills is a challenge. The markets are small and stuffed to the gills. If you want toilet paper or napkins or tissues, you need to find someone to get it down from a shelf. Plus, there are many elderly people in the neighborhood, and one must negotiate walkers as well as shopping carts and store employees who are kneeling on the floor to restock the shelves. There are also people who talk to themselves and shout obscenities—and no, they're not on invisible cell phones.

Yesterday I was quite sad, as Allen had decided to return to California. My brother dropped him off at the airport. That evening, my mother wanted orange sherbet, and because of her situation I felt duty-bound to find it, but it took a trip to five stores to find it. I finally got lucky in an Italian ice store. It felt like a miracle, like the song "Scarlet Ribbons." Then when I was in store number four, Allen called my cell phone. His flight was canceled (because of an impending snowstorm), and he was returning. When he walked in the door, I cried.

I don't usually talk like this, but I told him that perhaps this was God's way. We had a lovely Shabbat dinner (in my mother's apartment) and then walked around the corner to services at the Reform Temple of Forest Hills. When (the rabbi) marched past us with the Torah scroll, he stopped and asked how my mother was. I was quite touched.

As the journey continued, each day brought new twists, new turns. This next note, (written on February 12, 2006) is an honest one, but not pretty. I wrote it because I knew I would never remember what we were going through. Perhaps it would help somebody else who is experiencing this transition.

This morning, while I was still in bed, my mother told my brother and the aide that she wanted her children to help her commit suicide. She was told that we would keep her out of pain but would not help her end her life. She became angry.

Later, she became more mellow. Either she was going through a passage or hallucinating because of the medication. She began talking, saying that what she was going through was not like anything else she had experienced. She asked me what it was. I told her it was a passage. She also wanted to know if anybody else had ever gone through this. We told her yes, many had. She said her mind wasn't working, she was seeing things. I asked her what she saw. She opened her eyes and said, "I see you (my brother and myself) and Dad." I asked her if she saw her parents and grandparents. Yes, she did. Then she talked about having baskets on her neck, like pirate ships. She also complained that her legs are heavy, and she cannot move them. But she was, in fact, moving her legs, and was quite frenetic.

Then, most strange of all, she asked who put the sneakers in the refrigerator? My brother and I put our hands over our mouths, chuckling. When I went into the living room where Allen was working, he (in inimitable Allen fashion) said, "I did." Later he told me that he took his sneakers out of the refrigerator.

Allen and I sang a little to Mom today—and she was OK, unless we sang anything overtly religious, and then she gave us a hand motion to "change the channel." But we did sing "Eili, Eili" in Hebrew and English, and she was okay with that. Mother has no use for God talk, and she has made it clear to us, even now, that she does not believe in God. So, it is up to us as humans to ease her passage—and, to paraphrase Allen's mother, "God give me strength!"

My brother has pink eye, which is getting better. Mine is still bad. To say we are weary would be an understatement. Allen goes back to California on Monday. I rebooked my flight for Friday. It can't go on much longer, can it?

Sunday, February 13, 2006 (our sixth wedding anniversary, uncelebrated):

Today was difficult. My mother has grown weaker and weaker, yet somehow, she hangs on, albeit by a thread. People call and want updates, yet I can't give them any. How long is not much longer?

We're in the midst of a snowstorm now, and Allen and I took a brief walk while the clothes were in the washing machine. It wasn't that cold earlier, but it's expected to get colder, and stormier.

Meanwhile, Allen and I made return reservations for Monday, February 20— which will put my stay here at a month . . . Also, Allen badly needs shoulder surgery, and is in considerable pain, but that will have to wait. I'm so grateful to have him by my side.

On February 20, Allen flew back to California, by himself. Three days later, on February 23, Mother died, and Allen flew back to New York the following day.

The following email was written shortly after Mother died:

"She's going," Una said, as my brother and I rushed into the bedroom, where Mother lay in a cotton hospital gown, her legs encased in odd blue boots to prevent bedsores.

Una went into the den to pack her things and change into her street clothes. Her work was finished. So was Mother's, all but the last labored breaths.

My brother and I sat on either side of the hospital bed in her bedroom, watching, listening to the rhythm of her breaths, feeling her arms and legs.

Dying, said the social worker, is hard work, as if to console Mother who wanted it over with quickly. "Toss me out the window," she had told me earlier that week.

"From the twenty-fourth floor? I don't think so," I said.

She'd had enough. As I administered increasing doses of morphine under her tongue, alternating with spoons of lemon sherbet and occasional attempts at conversation, I wondered how long.

Not long, the visiting nurse said. Death, she said, begins with the feet, inching up the legs, rising up the torso to the head, where all that remains are a few vestigial releases of air. We keep vigil, get through the last ceremonies, including a frigid February graveside service, and we move on. But the disembodied souls stay with us until we take our last breaths.

The day of Mother's death, my eyes began to fail, the result of an infection that my brother and I had perhaps caught from Mother. Her parting gift, I quipped. When it came time to make the phone calls, I couldn't read the address book on my cell phone, couldn't read the eulogy I had prepared weeks before, couldn't do crossword puzzles or read the newspaper. Only the headlines.

Suddenly the doorbell rang. The undertakers? No, the good-looking young man was alone. He had come to pick up his mother, Una, and her suitcase.

Moments later, the undertakers arrived in crisp uniforms, like bellmen. They took her down through the back elevator. I hoped nobody would see. She wouldn't have liked that.

Sunday, February 26, the day of the graveside service and memorial, was bitter cold. Because my eyes were so badly infected, I had printed out my eulogy in 16-point type:

It's never been easy being told that I look exactly like my mother, because while the resemblance is strong, my mother, as I'm fond of saying, was a duchess in a former lifetime. She had an elegance and grace that I will never have, and she remained a lady long after the concept of lady went out of the popular lexicon.

When I told her my theory, my mother's sharp-as-a-tack response was, "If I was a duchess, how come I'm not rich?"

I retorted, "Because you married the court jester."

I am a product of that marriage, and despite my appearance, I'm more like the jester than the duchess. If my hair, makeup, or clothing were not up to my mother's standards, she would not mince words. Even when she was bedridden in the hospital, she said, "Janet, where do you get those hats? I wish I could get up and take you shopping."

Throughout her life, Mother detested prejudice. In 1950, when I was seven, we drove South for the first time. When I saw the signs on the water fountains that read "white only" and "colored only," I asked her what they meant. I never forgot her answer, and her concern that such injustice still prevailed in the United States. It shook her, as it did me.

During her final days with hospice at home, I told her that Una said that we were such a nice family, and we weren't at all prejudiced, like some people she had worked for. My mother smiled and said, "I don't see a color line. Do you?" I responded that when one is sick and being treated nicely, the only color is kindness.

My mother raised us with an absolute sense of right and wrong. In her final weeks, we talked about forgiveness. I mentioned several people and asked her if she forgave them. Her answer was always affirmative. But when I got to George W. Bush, she shook her head and said, "Never." Then I asked about Rudy Giuliani. "That bastard," she said. "What he did to his wife!"

In her final weeks, Mother decided she had had enough. She was ready. Although she was not fond of religious talk, when I recalled the verse from Ecclesiastes, "To everything there is a season," it resonated with her. But when she lived a couple of weeks longer than we had anticipated, I said, "For a woman who has made up her mind, you're sure taking your time."

"I fooled you," she said, and we shared a laugh. Mother wanted to finish her life as she had lived it, with dignity, with love, and with humor. And that is how she would like to be remembered.

I share these stories of our parents' last moments because I'm thinking of our own legacies. Allen and I are both products of our parents, of the values they passed on to us. As Allen frequently says when asked why we attend funerals, visit the sick, bring food to the mourners or those who are laid up, those mitzvahs are our commandments. But we also laugh a lot, and that laughter keeps us going.

CHAPTER 26

MAKING CHANGES

1965–

I don't remember much from my introductory class in microeconomics, but the concept of opportunity costs struck home. Choosing one opportunity or plan of action involves forgoing another.

During my first marriage, I followed my husband from Ann Arbor, Michigan, to Rochester, New York, to Northern California. I put my career on a back burner as I deferred to his. That was the way things were done. A woman's career was something to "fall back on," just in case. Because men were viewed as the primary breadwinners, many women of my generation earned *PHT* (Putting Hubby Through) degrees and worked until the children came along. Then we fell back.

Betty Friedan's *The Feminine Mystique* may have been published in 1963, but women's liberation didn't have a major impact on the job market until the 1970s. In the early 1960s, corporations placed male graduates into executive trainee programs. Women? We were secretaries. At the University of Michigan, where "student wife" was stamped on my job application, I couldn't find a professional-level job. In 1974, at age thirty-one, I finally got my journalism career off the ground. Mind you, I was slotted into a beat as a fashion editor, but my career evolved.

Then divorce brought other opportunities, and upheavals. When we sold our home in the suburbs, I cut my ties to the community where I had raised my children. When I remarried and moved to Silicon Valley, I gave up a measure of independence to become part of a couple. Marriage brought benefits. When I met Allen, I didn't even own a mobile phone. I'm surprised the techies even let my 1991 Toyota Tercel cross the Dumbarton Bridge to Silicon Valley. But moving to his home brought disruption and loneliness. At first, Allen traveled frequently for business, leaving me alone in a house that wasn't mine. Like the biblical matriarch Ruth, who follows mother-in-law Naomi to the land of their late husbands, I was living amid alien corn.* The family with whom we got together were his relatives because they lived locally. The choir I was singing with was his choir. And the friends we saw were mostly his friends.

Because the commute on a Friday night was problematic, I resigned from my Alameda synagogue and joined Congregation Beth Am in Los Altos Hills, where neither of us knew many people. But as newcomers, we made new friends together. We joined the synagogue choir that sang during the High Holidays, and we cofounded a new year-round Jewish community choir. We also became part of a *chavurah*, a friendship group of people around our age. With these new friends, we could share holidays and celebrations, as well as provide support during illness and mourning. Later we launched a discussion group to focus on issues of aging, and we also joined a couples' book group.

Synagogue friends in an interfaith marriage launched a study-social group that brought together Christians and Jews, and our friendship circle grew. We also joined new friends in Christian Bible study, lending a Jewish perspective

---

* John Keats, "Ode to a Nightingale."

to Christian scripture. In the process, we learned that while Christians, by and large, agree on key doctrines, notably the divinity of Jesus, they are far from monolithic. Some believe in the virgin birth, some don't, and many take issue with biblical literalism and with literal interpretations of the words of Leviticus. Some are loving parents of gay children, and two Christian men, both previously married to women, invited us to share their wedding celebration in church.

Life is fluid. Had I stood in one place, my life would have changed, regardless. I still meet Alameda friends Mary and Judy for lunch occasionally. But the other members of our women's group are gone. Kara remarried and moved to Montana. Marcia, who moved to Seattle to be near her daughter, died of lung cancer. Marilyn, a therapist who launched the women's group, moved back to Delaware to be near her children. Two others dropped out. Meanwhile, Mary and I, who were both single when the group started in 1996, are now remarried to husbands who are older and have health issues. We can't expect our world, or our bodies, to stay the same as we age.

When I married Allen, my world and my extended family grew, with two stepdaughters and four grandchildren from his side whom I see far more often than my own more distant blood relatives. I always have an invitation to my stepdaughter's raucous family Christmas dinners. Christmas Eve we often join Jewish friends for a Chinese dinner. By contrast, I remember one miserable Christmas Eve in Alameda when I cried myself to sleep.

Had I stayed in Alameda, I don't know how my life would have worked out. But I took a chance. So did Ruth the Moabite. According to scripture, Ruth became the great-grandmother of King David.

When I was a child, my mother listened to a radio soap opera, *The Romance of Helen Trent*, which offered hope to so-called older women. Before each episode, the announcer posed the rhetorical question, "Can love come to a woman after thirty-five?" How about fifty-seven? But expect opportunity costs. Like Ruth, you may need to move.

CHAPTER 27

I DIDN'T MARRY HIS HOUSE

2008–2009

"*I* liked where you used to live," my mother repeated practically until the day she died. She didn't hesitate to let me know that Allen's house and its furnishings were not to her taste. "It has a nice backyard, but I wouldn't want to live there."

I, too, liked where I used to live, where I could walk around the lagoons or picnic by San Francisco Bay, but Allen's work and his extended family were in Silicon Valley. My commute to San Francisco from Silicon Valley took longer than from Alameda, but it was doable. I made the move, but that didn't stop me from kvetching about the house. In the words of Allen's brother, Jerry, who used to bring bagels for Sunday breakfasts at our harvest-gold Formica breakfast table, "It's ugly!"

The house had myriad problems: An uninviting front entrance with a blank wall where a window should be, surrounded by spiny plants that attacked me as I opened the door. A rickety driveway. Inadequate closets. A master bathroom thirty-nine steps from the bedroom. A dark family room, a somber living room.

On the other hand, the gardens in front and in back had potential. A cottage behind the house brought in income. The neighborhood, with flat, walkable streets and well-groomed homes, offered two libraries and parks nearby, plus a theater and a small art museum.

Turning Allen's house into our house was a gradual process, reminding me of E. E. Cummings's poem "Spring is like a perhaps hand." Things shifted slowly, "changing everything carefully . . . / without breaking anything."

It took me awhile to buy in, not only financially but emotionally. At first, it was Allen's house, albeit with my books, computer, and living room furniture, but I felt like a boarder. As I tackled the front garden while Allen was on a business trip, the house slowly became mine.

"You have a color scheme!" said Allen's younger daughter, as she surveyed the front garden, where I had planted cherry-colored zinnias and blue salvia, adding hot pink and purple cyclamen in the shaded areas.

"Plants, like people, let you know where they're happy," said Carl, who formerly rented the cottage behind our house.

The gold Formica countertops and matching tabletop hit the chopping block early in our marriage, along with dog-disfigured carpeting. While our kitchen cabinets were being refinished, my husband stood at the supermarket checkout, peering over the pile of microwavable dinners in our cart. In his resonant voice, he announced to all within earshot, "I married my wife because she said she's a gourmet cook, and just look at what we're eating now!"

After we tackled the kitchen, we reexamined the nondescript exterior. The midcentury California ranch had grown piecemeal through several remodels, but it lacked a united front. Often, I drove right past the house. It did not welcome me. No picture window, no center of interest, no focus whatsoever.

"This house needs a face," I told Allen. "It should have a picture window."

"Do you want to take out the pantry cabinets and put in a picture window with a view into the washing machine?"

"Hmm. I guess not," I said. "How about a fake window? Maybe a mural?"

He was open to the possibility. But before we could tackle cosmetics, more substantial changes were needed. A retired architect in San Diego created a couple of sketches for us. The house would never make *Architectural Digest*, but it could be charming, in the country-cottage genre. Thomas Kincaid? I shuddered.

The architect suggested that we move a window, elongate the porch, add steps, change the front patio, redo the rutted blacktop driveway, and replace the cracked concrete front patio. We chose pavers in shades of bluish gray and reddish pink, which a contractor installed in a herringbone pattern. We repainted the yellow-beige exterior a bluish gray, choosing plum for the shutters. We found a wooden garden bench for the porch for thirty-five dollars. But the house still needed a focus.

During the Palo Alto Art and Wine Festival, we stumbled upon Stephen Schubert, a Southern California artist who created wooden trompe l'oeil dioramas with shutters opening to Tuscan landscapes. Since I had spent time in Italy, his designs captivated me.

"What do you think?" I asked Allen.

A couple of months later, our house had a cheerful face, welcoming me home and adding character to a previously anonymous California ranch. Suddenly, it had the ambience of an Italian villa.

The changes enhanced the home's curb appeal, but as we moved from midlife into the so-called "young old," cosmetic changes were not enough. We needed to improve the lighting, make the existing rooms more usable and accessible, and add grab rails and other safety features to the bathrooms.

Allen and I compiled a letter to an architect, numbering our concerns:

1. Our bedroom is too far from the bathroom, especially for folks who awaken at 3:00 a.m. The master bath has a scratched pink

tub, yellow-green walls, and old linoleum floors. It is also back-to-back with another bathroom, and if you open one medicine chest, you could practically peer into the other, reminiscent of the old Right Guard commercial.

2. The second bathroom has a claustrophobic shower with cracked tiles in a hideous cornflower blue that doesn't harmonize with the brick-colored floor.

3. The family room is dark and uninviting. Perfect for storing books, but who would want to read there?

4. The living room is huge, dark, and unwelcoming, and its feng shui is in retrograde. The ceiling is too low. With a fireplace on one wall, cabinetry on another, and patio doors directly opposite the entrance to the home, we have no good place to anchor furniture. The living room has plenty of seating, but nobody wants to sit there.

5. The makeshift closet in the master bedroom is little more than a cabinet, and it is so dark that I sometimes leave the house wearing mismatched shoes.

6. Since I write and edit at home, I need an office.

7. We do not need a family room. We do not need a home theater, a playroom, or a wine cellar. We do not need more space. We need to make better use of the space we have.

The architects agreed. The never-used fireplace needed to go. Ditto the family room, which we would sacrifice for a decent bathroom, better accessibility to the bedroom, and a walk-in closet. A former bathroom would become my office. The living room ceiling would be raised and illuminated with a skylight, and additional skylights would brighten the other rooms. With the proceeds from the sale of my townhouse, I paid for the renovation and now owned a share of the house.

The architect warned us to expect stress along the route to renovation. She and her partner emphasized, "We are not marriage counselors." Having been through a major remodel with my ex, I understood. I also knew what it was like to share my home with strangers for weeks at a time. This time, I hoped, a sense of humor would pull us through. That said, we got along fine with one another throughout, but we sometimes had issues to work out with the architect and contractor. Mistakes were made, and our former hall closet became the forgotten linen closet. Instead of a coat closet, we now had an unusual walk-through closet between the hallway and my office. It intrigued grandkids who circled the house playing hide and seek.

Raising the ceiling in the living room meant clearing out the attic, home to decades of photos, books, unused gifts from two weddings, and mementoes from our parents and our now-grown kids. It cost me two hundred dollars to send my son's yearbooks and school memorabilia to his home in England. Cartons of books went to Friends of the Library. The fireplace set, patio door blinds, and excess furniture were dispatched via Freecycle. Other stuff went to Goodwill. We crammed furniture into a large pod, or storage container, that the workers placed on the front lawn, along with a portable toilet and a dumpster.

From eight in the morning until five in the evening, the burly contractors broke walls, pulled out a ceiling, removed the fireplace, and cleared out one bathroom at a time. As a result, we were able to remain in the house throughout the ordeal. We moved our offices temporarily to a storage room off the garage, which unfortunately was not convenient to a bathroom.

Even when I was in the house, my path to the bathroom was obstructed by a polyethylene sheet, behind which lay a three-inch snowfall of old insulation mixed with God knows what. Not knowing what to do, I exited the house through a back door and walked to the front in bedroom slippers. En route, I was once caught in a cloudburst, but I couldn't get through the front door. Just inside the entrance, two masked men stood on ladders atop a sea of fallen insulation. My trip to the bathroom would have to wait.

As work progressed, the cavernous living room became even more cavernous.

We could peer into the attic, which had a temporary catwalk instead of a floor. At one point, we could see the sky. The fireplace became a hole in the wall, with a view of the water heater on the other side. One bathroom had holes in the floor.

With so much open area, we couldn't turn the heat on. During a cold spell, I walked around the house wearing a ski hat, a muffler, a windbreaker, and gloves. One night, it was so cold that we hopped into bed at 8:00 p.m. and turned on the electric blanket. For a couple of months, we lived in two rooms separated from the construction by polyethylene sheeting.

Then the painting began. It took eight samples and repeated trips to the paint store to find the right shade for the living room, a color that would work both day and night. I finally settled on an ice blue that Kelly Moore calls Dim Sum. After another few stabs, I selected Quiche Lorraine for the guest bathroom. Who dreams up these names? Meanwhile, one of the contractors shamed us into replacing our carpeting and all our doorknobs, adding to the costs.

"You don't want this to look like a remodel, do you?" he said.

We also replaced all the blinds and organized our new closets with shelving and modular units that my husband and his brother installed. The contractors, both well over six feet, were puzzled when we asked them to rearrange two poles in the walk-in closet to accommodate the clothing of shorter people. I needed to be able to reach the higher pole for jackets and shirts, but I also wanted the lower pole to be high enough for hanging pants and skirts full length. That's a request they'd never encountered. However, these days, I have a little stepstool in the closet to accommodate my shrinking height.

Meanwhile, Allen's brother wanted a room named after him, so an extra toilet room, housed in the alcove that once held the fireplace, became the Jerry. We covered it with a rainforest wallpaper mural. The Jerry, which could never pass for a powder room, has no mirror or conventional sink. However, it contains an Allen-rigged toilet/sink arrangement with a top that spouts warm water when the toilet is flushed—a conversation piece.

The last stage of the remodel involved refinishing the hardwood floors, and we had to evacuate. We came back from a week in New York to find "Do not enter" signs on all our doors, forcing us to seek refuge with friends. Then came the restoration. With help from Tim, we emptied the pod, piece by piece.

When the pods were cleared away, they left ugly brown rectangles on what used to be our lawn. They inspired us to kill the lawn altogether and landscape with water-resistant plants.

Living in a limited space for several months reminded me that we take up more space than we need, and we don't use our space well. Growing up in New York, I had friends who lived in one-bedroom apartments, sharing a room with one or more siblings while their parents slept in the living room. They considered themselves fortunate because they were in America, where they were safe.

After several months of banging and chaos, I found peace and quiet again. I'm surrounded by color, I have light, and I have books, a piano, and an office of my own. I'm also grateful for the presence of the Jerry, the spare WC. It prevents Allen and me from colliding with one another at 3:00 a.m. That's a bump our marriage has not had to endure.

I'm only sorry that my mother never saw our new old house. She would have kvelled (Yiddish for *gushed*). Then she would have shaken her head at the Jerry, which she would only use in an emergency. She also would have wondered what we were thinking when we put in a quirky walk-through closet. I might tell her we installed it to amuse the grandkids.

CHAPTER 28

MR. FIX-IT'S APPRENTICE*

2002–present

After I remarried, I hung on to my Alameda townhouse for a couple of years. To play it safe, I rented it out, ironically, to a man who had once answered my singles ad. After two years, I felt secure enough in the marriage to put my townhouse on the market, but first I needed to paint, spruce up the planter boxes, and make sure everything worked. That's why I took down the broken track for a vertical blind assembly and put it in the backseat of my car. My plan was to have it packaged and shipped to the factory in Oregon.

A couple of days later, when Allen picked me up at the Caltrain station, he informed me, "Oh, by the way, I fixed your blind assembly."

"You fixed it? How did you do that?" I said, incredulously.

"I just happened to have the spare parts in the garage."

---

* A version of this story ran in *J. The Jewish News of Northern California* on February 9, 2023.

That'll teach me to stop nagging him about the state of the garage, which I rarely enter. I'm afraid I won't be able to find my way out amid tools of various vintages, discarded hoses, pipe fittings, wood scraps, bicycles, and spare rolls of toilet paper. From time to time, I suggest that we do a cleanup, but since I have respiratory allergies, Allen advises against it. He'll get to it, he says.

But because he saved me the cost of the shipping and repair on my blind assembly, and countless other projects for which ordinary folks would have called a repair person, I have learned to accept Allen's quirks.

On three occasions, General Electric sent repair crews to determine why our microwave didn't operate in the convection mode. One of them told me it was unreasonable to expect the oven to reach 400 degrees in less than an hour. Meanwhile, GE sent us replacement parts that fixed nothing.

The third visit from GE was a charm, but the fixer was Allen. While the innards of the oven were exposed, Allen poured the technician a glass of water and looked at the assembly himself. Interestingly, the oven's thermostat and heating element were practically touching, preventing the oven from reaching 400 degrees in a reasonable amount of time. After the technician left without solving the problem, Allen took apart the oven. He used a piece of aluminum from a discarded coffee can as an improvised shield. Then he wrote a letter of explanation to GE, which rewarded him by extending the warranty and sending him another oven lightbulb. Ironically, we were the first consumers to report the problem.

Living with Mr. Fix-It is an adventure, and these adventures magnify when we travel: He has fixed errant screen doors, sticky drawers, and intermittent burners in a relative's home, in a French friend's flat—and even in an Airbnb. Pre-Allen, the men in my life were not fixers. My father, a World War II veteran who was saved from combat by his typing skills, used to boast that he had the lowest mechanical aptitude in the history of the US Army. My first husband, who did not inherit the handyman gene, might delay repairs until his father's visit or ask me to call an electrician or a plumber. Sometimes I would tackle a repair job myself, using a do-it-yourself book written by women. That's how I learned to rewire a lamp. Hardware stores could be a challenge. When I asked questions, a crusty old gentleman wearing a shop apron would find the part he thought I needed without telling me how to use it. He would invariably say, "Your husband will know what to do!"

Stifling my laughter, I would respond, "Maybe, but if you explain it to me so I can understand it, I can explain it to him."

The salesman would shake his head in frustration and then explain the process slowly.

That do-it-yourself experience came in handy when I became Mr. Fix-It's apprentice. When our two-year-old dishwasher began flashing an *F11* error message, I consulted the manual, which informed me that *F11* means the dishwasher won't drain—something we'd already figured out. Then we watched a short repair video on YouTube. It looked like an easy fix. We followed the steps: Remove the lower spray arm, check the holes for clogs. Remove the filter system and clean it thoroughly. Scoop out the water. Remove the nonreturn valve and rinse it. Spin the impeller several times in both directions. Then put everything back. We did all that, but the onerous *F11* signal flashed again.

Time to call customer service? You've got to be kidding! In the garage, Mr. Fix-It found an old plastic hose and inserted it into the little plastic valve that sits above the sink. It's called the dishwasher air gap, but I have no idea what it does, other than occasionally gush water all over the counter. Then he found an improvised fitting in the plumbing drawer and mated it with the hose. He screwed the fitting onto the faucet and forced the hose down the air gap. Following that, he backflushed the dishwasher drain line through the air gap, creating a puddle in the bottom of the dishwasher. The only things that burbled to the surface were one or two measly rosemary needles. We bailed out the water, put everything back together, and ran a short cycle. The dishwasher drained. We have no idea what we fixed.

Once the dishwasher was working again, we noticed that the white plastic air gap was crumbling. Allen found a stunning turquoise one online. We cleared the mess under the sink, removed the old air gap, and attempted to connect the new one. As I stood at the sink, Allen lay on the floor, calling out orders: "I need a 5/16 wrench. No, I need a 3/16. Just hand it to me. Okay, I'm going to feed the new air gap through the hole. Tell me when you can grab the turquoise contraption. You got it?"

"It's crooked," I said. "You need to angle it to your left. Sorry, to your right. Now what?"

I screwed the white plastic nut to the turquoise thing and topped it with a gleaming new steel cover. Mission accomplished. But Allen stayed on the floor. He couldn't get up. He looked up at me, laughed, and said, "Bring me a pillow. I need a nap."

CHAPTER 29

A HOLE IN OUR HEARTS BEGINS TO HEAL

1999—

Three-year-old Tim first arrived at my Alameda condo on his grandfather's shoulders, carrying a red Teletubby doll on a keychain. Allen introduced me as Granny Janny, and the name stuck. For me, it was love at first sight. On weekends, we became a threesome, taking Tim on walks along the Alameda shore and to services at my synagogue, where he looked forward to being our ring bearer.

The morning of the wedding, my mother said to him, "Isn't it wonderful! You're getting a new grandma today."

"Granny Janny already is my grandma," he replied.

While Tim was a bit squirmy during the wedding ceremony, he loved the reception, where he could cut loose. Before the wedding cake was served, he made sure to test it, dipping his fingers into the yellow buttercream frosting. When he saw the picture that captured his handiwork, he laughed. "I did that," he said.

After we returned from our honeymoon, we picked up Tim and greeted our friends at services in Alameda. "Will you look at them!" Josh shouted out. "Married for less than a month, and they already have a child!"

Then Tim wanted to know when Allen and I were going to have a child together. "We already have children," we told him. "Besides, we were too old, but not too old to be your grandparents."

Tim is the child of a single mother who juggled two jobs while also completing her bachelor's degree. To help her out, and because we enjoyed being with Tim, he spent many evenings and weekends with us when he was small. His father, who weaved in and out of his life, had moved out of the area.

When Tim was little, Allen loved reading *The Little Prince* to him at bedtime, remarking that the rose is special because the prince loves her, just as Tim is special because we love him. We also watched videos together. In *Babe*, the story about a precocious pig, Tim learned about "the way things are": farmers keep pigs to fatten them up for Christmas dinner, and Pig Paradise, from which no pig ever returns, is to be avoided. Another favorite, *Stuart Little*, struck a chord. Stuart, an anthropomorphic mouse adopted by a human family, deeply misses his biological parents, saying there's a hole in his heart. Tim looked at us and said there's a hole in his heart because he missed his father.

When we celebrated Allen's seventy-fifth birthday, Tim got up and grabbed a mic, saying Allen was the father he wished he had.

Tim relished my cooking, adding vanilla at every opportunity because he loved the aroma. He also enjoyed peeling apples with a hand tool and then eating the peels. One day I made meatloaf. Tim told me he loved to make meatloaf himself. I told him how I made it—with spices, breadcrumbs, egg, and maybe Worcestershire sauce—and asked him how he made it.

"I take the package out of the freezer and put it in the microwave," he said.

Over the years, we took Tim to Yosemite; to a cross-cultural family camp involving American Jews, Israelis, and Palestinians; and to Disneyland. Allen camped with him in Death Valley, and we sent Tim to a sleepaway farm camp that his aunt had enjoyed as a child. There he took care of animals he had seen only in petting zoos and theme parks. While he cried in the car on the way to camp, when he arrived and saw the animals, his eyes brightened: "This isn't at all what I thought it would be," he said, waving goodbye. The next year, he hopped on the bus, greeted by counselors who knew him, and he was glad to be on his way.

When Tim was in his twenties, his father welcomed him to his home in another city. For three years, we didn't see our grandson, and for the better part of two years, nobody in our family did. He didn't answer our emails or our texts. He didn't cash our birthday checks. Then the coronavirus struck, and since we were in a high-risk category because of our age, we couldn't visit him. However, his mother and his aunt were eventually able to visit him, sending us texts with photos, telling us he was fine. Nonetheless, we were the ones with a hole in our hearts.

Then, at age twenty-five, Tim moved back into his mother's home and back into our lives, sharing the hugs we had missed for years. He was with us for Father's Day at our house, when he, his mother, and his aunt prepared all the food. After my brother had surgery, Tim helped him negotiate the steps from house to patio and back, and when my brother moved to a senior residence, Tim helped him settle in. When we need help with various household projects, Tim steps in gladly. In his midtwenties, Tim has become a mensch, but his career plans are still up in the air. We keep our fingers crossed.

These days, we don't talk about the lost years. But we told Tim that we never gave up on him. With hope, that hole in our hearts is healing.

CHAPTER 30

MY BROTHER'S KEEPER

2001–2021

*I*n the summer of 2001, when my father lay in hospice care, he said, "I know you'll look after your brother."

I nodded. "You know I will. Don't worry."

I think I may have been born to be a big sister, but until I was nine and a half, I was an only child. When I was seven, my mother gave birth to a boy on a Monday who died on a Friday. I never saw him. Two and a half years later, I was in the car when she brought my tiny new brother home. We greeted his arrival as a gift from heaven. I relished my role as live-in babysitter and entertainer, teaching him songs and amusing him with puppet shows. Later, he entertained us, orchestrating dinner table shows in which he was the emcee, introducing each of his "guests" with aplomb. My mother hammed up "Out of My Dreams" from *Oklahoma!* while my father arose for a Jimmy Durante–style vaudeville routine. Sometimes I would join him, or I'd sing "Wouldn't It

Be Loverly." Then my brother would do a command performance of "Torero." Since he didn't know Spanish, he sang what he thought he heard: "Gay knocka deecka stinky hockadoo, mishkolando, polando, turkey woomly gar." We would end the show in hysterics.

My brother was the child who could cheer us up. He was also the devoted child who didn't rebel, as I had done. While I moved to upstate New York and later California, he returned to New York City after college, and he was there for my parents throughout their long illnesses. He was the one who phoned when it was time for me to hop on a plane. Although he never married and had children, he was deeply devoted to my two children, who became counselors in the camp where he was executive director.

When he reached his mid-thirties, he developed serious neurological problems, which were misdiagnosed for many years. Initially, he thought he might have a skin disease because he developed lesions on his left hand. Later he realized he had burned himself and hadn't felt the pain because he'd lost sensation in his left hand; his left arm had only about twenty-five percent functionality. His piano-playing days were over. For my brother, who loved to play at gatherings for friends and family, that was major. But other changes were even more dire.

He had a tumor in his spinal cord. Although it was benign, it seriously impacted his mobility and had to be removed. About a year after that surgery, his neck became unstable, and he required two more procedures. Then arthritis set in, affecting his mobility.

Business failures complicated the situation. For years, my brother worked with my father as book distributors, but bad decisions and a declining market led to the closing of their business. When my father retired, my brother was forced to regroup. He became the executive director of a camp for disadvantaged youth from New York City. Unfortunately, internal disputes and funding shortfalls closed the eighty-five-year-old camp, which at one point had served 1,200 children. After that, he held several jobs, the last of which was for a Long

Island title company. When the boss died, leaving the business in shambles, my brother was once again out of work.

In 2016, his plan to rent a condo in Florida fell through just as the lease on his Long Island apartment was expiring. Allen and I talked over the situation, and he invited my brother to stay with us "until he could get his feet on the ground." Putting his furniture into storage on Long Island, my brother arrived in time for Thanksgiving 2016. None of us suspected that our threesome would be on a five-year plan.

CHAPTER 31

FIGURING OUT HOW TO USE THE TV IS A REMOTE POSSIBILITY*

2021

A decade ago, my husband wanted a large-screen TV for the living room, so he spent days checking websites in search of the best deal.

"Enough already," I said, exasperated. "It's Father's Day. Go ahead and buy it."

Well, he ran out that afternoon and came home with a fifty-two-inch Samsung. Ten years later, I figured out how to turn it on. Maybe by next year I'll be able to watch a movie all by myself.

Listen, I am no Luddite, and long ago I learned how to use a VCR as well as a CD player. These days, I help friends deal with the quirks of Microsoft Word and assist choir members with audiovisual recording and transmission. But

---

* An earlier version of this story ran March 24, 2021, in *J. The Jewish News of Northern California.*

those skills don't help me with the television, particularly since we have four remotes on the coffee table and another five stashed away in a drawer.

"Why are those five remotes in a drawer if we never use them?" I asked my husband.

Allen shrugged. "You don't need to worry about them," he said. "You only need to concern yourself with what's on the coffee table. The one that's shaped like a dog bone is the one that turns on the TV."

I fingered the remotes on the coffee table. Not one of them, in my estimation, looked like a dog bone. This process wasn't getting any easier. Some time ago, I had asked Allen to provide a one-page user manual. I found it in the drawer with the remotes we never use. I had never looked at it, or if I did, I probably shook my head and put it back in the drawer. Here's what it said:

"Normal TV watching procedure:

"Turn on everything with pink remote." That's the universal remote, which has pink tape around the edges so I can identify it.

"Use only the Comcast remote for everything except on/off . . . talk to it. If you turn on everything with the Comcast remote, it will not turn on the receiver, and the sound will not work as designed. If you do not aim any remote at the glass dome over the French candle, it may not work right.

"When all else fails:

"Use pink remote. Turn off everything, turn on . . . AIM! Now use Comcast remote.

"Recording for future watching:

"On Comcast remote: Press guide and scan for channel, program, and time.

"Press red dot button on right above Pg prompt."

Yeah, right. The so-called pink-trimmed, one-size-fits-all universal remote is useless, Allen told me later. It never did what it's supposed to do. However, the Comcast remote, which turns the TV on and off, doesn't turn the sound on. For that, I need to grab another remote labeled Yamaha. Either that, or press the ON button on the Yamaha receiver, which is in the cabinet below the TV.

That much I get, sort of. But if Alexa, our electronic assistant, can turn the couch light on and off, play Nat King Cole, and deliver the news and the weather report, why can't she turn on the living room TV?

My brother called out, "Alexa, teach Janet how to use the remote."

"Sorry," she responded, "I'm not sure about that."

I'm not beyond learning. Heck, when we stayed at an Airbnb and the owners provided a sheet with directions, I had no problem following them to the letter. With that in mind, my brother created a more extensive tutorial, geared just for me.

Step 1: "Turn on TV using Comcast remote. Press all-power button on top right."

Step 2: "For sound: On remote labeled Audio (Yamaha), press button on right under yellow tape. Make sure receiver indicator shows *hdmi4* on the screen; it usually does. If not, call Allen or me."

Step 3: "For movies or programs: If you want Amazon Prime or Netflix, press Xfinity button in center of Comcast remote. A series of choices will come in. Move cursor toward the right and press Apps."

Step 4: (Gets more complicated.) "In Apps, more choices will come up. . . . Move cursor to desired choice and press. In both Netflix and Prime, an icon will appear with several names, including yours. Move cursor to your name and press. That should get you in. If some internet issues occur and the selection doesn't take, then wait it out . . . "

Step 5: "Finding a movie or program on Netflix or Amazon Prime requires a second tutorial."

For now, I use the uncomplicated small TVs in my bedroom and in the kitchen. As long as the batteries work, I have no problem finding CNN or *60 Minutes* or even *Masterpiece Theatre*. One of these days, I may try to watch a movie on the living room set, pressing the right buttons all by myself. However, that's for another day. I have too many books I want to read first.

Meanwhile, all this remote learning may be for naught.

"You know," Allen said, "if we buy a new TV, it will come equipped with Alexa, and she'll be able to handle everything."

CHAPTER 32

CAR MITZVAHS AND OTHER MILESTONES

1991, 2017

When I walked into Walnut Creek Toyota as a newly single mom, half-a-dozen nattily dressed salesmen, some swaggering with clunky jewelry, stood at the door.

"Which one of you doesn't smoke?" I asked.

The men snickered, clicking the taps on their heels, wondering if this brazen broad was a customer or a curiosity. Only one man raised his hand, a short, dark-haired guy.

"Okay," I said to him, "take me for a spin in a new Tercel."

I cloaked my ignorance under a façade of assertiveness as I had never purchased a car on my own, and I didn't talk car talk. I didn't know the difference between a power train and a choo-choo train, nor did I know a torque from a toque. But I had cash on hand, knew exactly what I wanted, and after visiting a couple of showrooms, I was determined not to go for another ride with a salesman who reeked of tobacco. I also brought along my friend Michael because I knew that a single woman in desperate need of an automobile was seen as an easy mark.

I knew the games car salesmen played in those days, sashaying back and forth between their cubicles and what they called the "sales manager's office," which was probably the bathroom. You'd make an offer, they'd leave the cubicle, they'd cross out your offer with a counteroffer, and then you'd counter again. I knew about high-balling and low-balling, and I didn't have time to play ball because I didn't have a drivable car. So I plunked down about ten grand, by the time taxes and fees were included, and I drove off a day or so later in a new 1991 Tercel.

The Tercel replaced a car that had given me nothing but trouble, a used 1985 Mitsubishi that became mine in the divorce settlement. In the fall of 1990, I replaced the transmission, to the tune of three grand. Then in February 1991, the Mitsubishi began spewing blue-and-purple smoke on the Bay Bridge as I drove home from San Francisco. Fellow drivers honked at me, pointing out the problem. I also saw the oil gauge on the dashboard flashing red. With a little luck, I thought I might make it over the bridge. Fortunately, I made it across the bridge and with a bit more luck, I pulled into my driveway.

I called Michael, who suspected the Mitsubishi service department of gross negligence. When I had taken the car in a few days before for a routine service, Michael guessed that the mechanic had drained the oil and failed to replace it. If the engine was fried, which another repair place confirmed later, I needed a new car. When I called Mitsubishi to complain, the service manager insisted there's no way they would have drained the car of oil and not replaced it. Besides, he said, it was an old car, on its last legs, with some ninety thousand miles on it. I told him I'd see him in small claims court. I did, and I lost.

During the interregnum between marriages, I relocated four times, accompanied by my trusty Tercel, which never required major service. My former boyfriend detested my two-door subcompact and never wanted to drive it. My mother said the cramped back seat was a torture chamber and getting in and out was brutal. But the car wasn't built for her or for my boyfriend. Easy to maneuver and easy to park, the Tercel was made for small people like me. That car was my baby, and I didn't tolerate trash talk, particularly from my mother.

After I remarried in 2000, I sold my townhouse, but I kept the car, which my husband called the Terkel. Well, if he could call my car a pejorative surname, I could address it with an affectionate nickname: how's Studs? Moving on to 2017, California's Cash for Clunkers program offered $1,000 to consumers willing to get cars like mine off the road. Since the automobile I had purchased twenty-six years before was old enough to have celebrated two car mitzvahs, I thought that was a good deal. However, with under one hundred thousand miles on it, the car was no clunker, and I cried when I relinquished it.

These days I drive a Prius, but to me it's just a car, a car I share with my husband. On the other hand, the Tercel was mine. We shared a history.

CHAPTER 33

THE SOUP GRANDMA*

1998–

When my first granddaughter was born and I boarded the plane to San Diego, an empty eight-quart soup pot came along for the ride. In my new role as Granny Janny the Soup Grandma, I wanted to ensure that baby Lindsay got a whiff of chicken soup, the stock that sustains us. While I made the soup with high hopes during my visit, Lindsay and her younger sister, Kelsey, were in college before my daughter attempted chicken soup from scratch. Although her matzah ball soup received kudos at her seder, she hasn't made it since. Meanwhile, neither of her daughters puts soup on their A-list.

Where did I go wrong?

Text from Lindsay, now a nurse: "I never really eat soup. I don't think I like it. . . . But I'm sure your soup is great!"

---

* A version of this story ran in *J. The Jewish News of Northern California* on April 19, 2023.

From Kelsey, then a college senior: "I don't dislike it, but I don't find anything special in it, except maybe Panera's soups."

From my daughter: "I love your homemade soup! Especially if it has noodles or rice in it."

However, both my stepdaughters and their children adore my chicken soup, and so do friends of all backgrounds. So maybe it's not a genetic thing at all.

I'd like to say the soups I make came out of my childhood memories, but they didn't come from my mother's kitchen, even though she loved homemade soup, nor from my grandmother's, as she was the only Jewish grandmother in my recollection who didn't cook. What I do remember is that when I was sick, a neighbor in the building would send over a pot of chicken soup. I might not have been able to recognize most of the ingredients, but I remember how the soup made me feel. These days, I am the soup-toting neighbor. The chicken soup may not be the stock of my childhood, but I hope it makes others feel better. I know it works for me. That's why I almost always have homemade stock in the freezer.

Now I own a stash of cookbooks, but I'm also an experimentalist, constantly trying to replicate a recipe based on a dim memory. But my soups never come out the same way twice. There are too many variables, including the chicken itself. I keep a bone bag in the freezer—yes, we collect bones after family dinners, but I'm a bit reluctant for our dinner guests to catch us in the act.

When I've amassed at least three pounds—a turkey carcass is the best—it's time to make stock. I fill a pot with water, toss in the bones, bring the pot to a boil, and add an array of root vegetables, herbs, and spices. When scum rises to the surface, I strain the stock and keep it simmering. After a couple of hours or more, I strain the stock again, this time removing all the bones and vegetables. Then I sauté more vegetables, add the stock and some cooked rice or barley, and call it soup. I may add leftover chicken or turkey at the last minute. Overcooked bird doesn't fly in my kitchen.

Unfortunately, noodles don't work terribly well either, unless you're going to eat it right away. When I was a child, my mother often served Campbell's chicken noodle soup for lunch, which I dubbed Frog Soup. Why? Small greenish-yellow globules floated to the surface, resembling lily pads, and in my childhood mind, lily pads meant frogs. The soup wasn't awful, but the noodles were too squishy. I preferred the tiny noodles in Lipton's soups, which my friend's mother made, but the stock was too salty, and the chicken was invisible. "Just because you can't see it, doesn't mean it's not there," Arthur Godfrey would say in his off-the-cuff pitches for Lipton's. But what part of a chicken is in a sulfur-colored clump or powder? The craw?

Meanwhile, I keep experimenting. Penzeys' Old World and Krakow Nights spice mixes help approximate some of the aromas I remember. I favor using parsnips, celery, carrots, onions, leeks, garlic, and soupçons of herbs from my garden. I tried to grow dill, but critters seem to polish it off before it lands in my soup, so I sometimes add fennel fronds, which look like dill. Some years ago, during a choral exchange, I watched a visiting chef from France add curry powder to my soup, so since then, I've followed suit. My favorite is Penzeys' Maharajah Curry Powder, which contains saffron.

My chicken soup is not like Grandma Sylvia's or Aunt Sadie's or Bubbie Frieda's, nor is it the soup my husband's mother made. She used chicken feet, which I can't find in the supermarkets around here, although I found a website that sells them for $16.95 a pound. In any case, I can't imagine putting feet into my soup, but you never know. One friend plunges a whole uncooked chicken into a pot of water. She then serves the soup with bones in the bowl as well as vegetables that have been cooked to oblivion. It is tasty, bringing up memories of the legendary Lindy's in New York, but it would not go over with my family. While I've been known to munch on the mushy carrots and chicken that cooked for hours, my husband likes his carrots crunchy and his poultry just cooked.

When I bring soup to sick friends or relatives, their praise is effusive, and they share their own childhood memories. But after my stepdaughter's first child was born, she commented on the "strange animal protein" floating in her bowl. Was it a fly? No, it was dark meat! Her family favors white meat, boneless and skinless. My other stepdaughter is freaked out by what she calls "carcass," and one year when I added giblets to the turkey gravy on Thanksgiving, both sisters freaked out, forcing me to strain the gravy before I brought it to the table. Now my husband gobbles the turkey giblets before they land in the soup.

However, I get no flak on my matzah ball soup since I use a clear stock with no visible animal innards. One Passover, riffing on Shakespeare, I penned the following verse after preparing matzah ball soup:

In the Soup
There is a tide in the affairs of chicken soup
Which, when taken at the full, leads to a clear and golden broth.
But when the roiling wrath of foam erupts,
Spreading its gray-brown murk atop a simmering stock,
One must grab a slotted spoon and skim the ooze,
Or one may forever bemoan the opportunity lost.
O that this too, too solid scum would melt, dissipate, disappear.
Alas, it's too, too late.
The tide has passed
The deed is done.

I emailed my verse to Elizabeth Zelvin, a high school classmate, writer, and psychotherapist, who is also known for her matzah ball soup.

She replied: *"Dear Janet, Call me a Philistine, but my immediate reaction was: You make it from scratch? Oy, am I impressed!"*

Soup is all about time, and while an Instant Pot or a pressure cooker can speed the process, soup is still a messy affair, what with shopping, chopping, and straining. Maybe that's why it's the province of grandmas like me.

Even if my genetic grandchildren are less than enthusiastic, I have plenty of appreciative relatives and friends in my extended family, for whom Passover isn't Passover without Granny Janny's matzah ball soup. What I'm really doing is creating memories. In the meantime, I recognize that everyone's tastes are different, so before you discard that carcass, send it my way. Ditto on the giblets.

CHAPTER 34

*GRANDPARENTS FROM MARS**

2007–

After two days of skiing in Tahoe, we were sprawled out, exhausted, on the couch of the rented condo. We were curled up with books, except for five-year-old Shelby, who was busily drawing. Then she rushed over to show us what she had done.

She had filled a piece of white cardboard with capital letters in various colors and sizes, some crossed out, some on top of one another. The first word was "BROO." A couple of lines down was "ELO HAY NOO." At the bottom, in pink, was "SHBT SHLOM."

This kindergartner, who isn't Jewish by any definition, is the child of my husband's older daughter. Shelby, who had often spent Shabbat with us, had written the Motzi blessing phonetically, and she was quite proud of herself.

---

* Some information was previously published in *J. The Jewish News of Northern California.*

So was I. I didn't know the Motzi, the blessing for bread, until I was almost nineteen.

Her cousin Ryan, the child of Allen's younger daughter, also isn't halachically Jewish. However, when he was three years old, Ryan was determined to keep an eternal light in my menorah, even though Hanukkah was long over. When he arrived at our house one winter day, the first thing he did was ask for the Tinkertoy, which has extra-wide plastic dowels and large wooden spools. Then he pointed to the dining room cabinet and said, "Menorah."

Assembling his tools, Ryan placed an orange dowel into the middle candleholder, topped it with a round wooden spool, and then fastened another dowel on top to form a tower. Before the whole assemblage toppled over, he announced in his toddler soprano, "This is the shamash. This is the shamash." Then he proceeded to fill all the candleholders.

As far as I know, Tinkertoy is not in the Judaica business. But Ryan was, in his own fashion. That menorah—a stunning Israeli chanukiah with wide candleholders fashioned from bullet shells—marks my own life passage. I purchased it with a gift certificate that my *Jewish Bulletin* colleagues gave me for my 1998 bat mitzvah. When Ryan was young, it did double duty.

So here I am, a self-taught Jew raised by secular parents who were raised by secular parents. As a young adult in a mixed marriage, I raised my own children Unitarian. Now, after turning to Judaism in midlife, I'm a Jewish grandma who must explain myself to grandchildren who aren't being raised Jewish. Talk about challenges.

The bagels, latkes, brisket, and matzah ball soup are the easy part. The blessings require explanation. While visiting my daughter's family recently, we happened to be dining out on a Friday night. It's their tradition to say grace before meals. Kelsey, then seven, put her hands together and closed her eyes, saying, "This is the way we pray."

I nodded, without putting my hands together.

My daughter asked if I would like to say the blessing. Since it was Shabbat,

Allen and I grabbed a roll from the breadbasket and began chanting the Motzi, giving everybody a chunk of bread at the conclusion.

"Jewish people sing their prayers?" Kelsey asked.

"Yes, we often do," I responded.

"Is that why you're Jewish?" said Lindsay, then nine.

Everybody laughed.

"No," I said. "We're Jewish because we were born Jewish."

On the other hand, maybe she has a point. Our chanting keeps us tied to our traditions in a way that words alone cannot.

When Kelsey was a little older, and we were sitting around our own dining room table, she popped out with, "Everybody, raise your hands if you're Jewish."

My son-in-law let her know her request wasn't appropriate. But years later, we're all able to laugh about it, including Kelsey.

In the grandparent pantheon, we are the weird ones, the ones who are different, and not every difference brings laughter, from them or from us. When Shelby became a teenager, she stopped going to services with us. She let us know that she loved Christmas and didn't want to be Jewish because Jews weren't supposed to celebrate Christmas.

We told her, as lovingly as we could, that we would never take Christmas away from her, or from anybody else. We are not Grinches, and we continue to give our children and grandchildren Christmas gifts. However, we don't decorate our house for the season, as we once did.

When Allen and I were first married, his older daughter was upset that we weren't putting up a tree.

"Can't you just have a little tree?" she asked me.

A little tree is like a little pregnant, I thought to myself. What I told her was that even though she didn't feel that the Christmas tree was particularly Christian, it still didn't belong in a Jewish home. I had made that decision for myself, back in 1988. After Allen and I were married, we agreed to host Passover, Thanksgiving, and Hanukkah. These days, Allen's younger daughter hosts

Christmas dinner, and we attend, along with his ex-wife and members of our extended family. It's a joyous time, and most recently, we all attended wearing pajamas and exchanged white elephant gifts.

However, one year when Allen's younger daughter spent the holidays in Tahoe, her sister had no place to go. Her children were spending time with their paternal relatives, and she was alone. I invited her to our home for Christmas dinner. Instead of a traditional turkey and sweet potato dinner, I think I served a standing rib roast and homemade cranberry-apple pie. Was I celebrating Christmas? No, I was helping her to enjoy her holiday.

In that spirit one year, Allen and I spent Christmas Eve serving food at a homeless shelter. After dinner, when the guests were bedding down in their sleeping bags, we began to lead Christmas carols. Several weeks later, my rabbi approached us in the social hall and said, "I heard what you did at the shelter. Thank you. There's more than one way to feed people."

I think feeding people is what we do best. Our kids and grandkids may not always understand our ceremonies—when Kelsey was three, she tried to blow out the Shabbat candles after the blessing, thinking the prayer was equivalent to singing "Happy Birthday"—and some may think Jewish is akin to Martian.

On the same visit, Lindsay wanted to know if we make pizza for lunch.

"No," I said. "I don't make pizza."

"Is that because you're Jewish?"

I laughed. "No, it's just not something I make. If I want pizza, we order it."

That was many years ago, and the conversation has become part of our family legends. In fact, these days, I have been known to make pizza, buying the dough from Trader Joe's and adding my own toppings. However, I still don't make it for lunch, and I don't add pepperoni. But with fresh heirloom tomatoes and basil from the garden, it's amazing.

Over the years, Allen and I have learned to live with being different, and it's not just our Judaism. As he has said for years, "My head is screwed on crooked. I hear things differently. I think differently." Do we think out of the box? Who needs a box? But despite our differences, we can always find something to bring our family together.

CHAPTER 35

PURGING A LIFETIME OF STUFF NOBODY WANTS*

2021

*I*f you think you're going to die, it's best to clean up first. It's bad enough to land in the emergency room with a safety pin in your underwear. But after you have been tucked away for eternity, do you really want your survivors to handle your ratty pink bathrobe?

You'd think I would have learned a lesson when a good friend died in 2014, and my husband was named executor of his estate. We inherited the detritus of three houses, including a 1910 family home that had been mostly vacant since his mother's death in 1998. Surrounded by trash, yearbooks from the 1920s, and old magazines and report cards piled on the living room floor, we plunged into a hundred years of dust-covered memories.

I couldn't find an "away" in the house, a place where items were neatly stored.

---

* An earlier version of this chapter appeared May 18, 2021, in *J. The Jewish News of Northern California*.

Nor could I find a trash receptacle, other than the Santa Claus wastebasket in the center of the living room floor. Amid the chaos, however, I found Emily Holt's *Everyman's Encyclopaedia of Etiquette: What to Write, What to Wear, What to Do, What to Say*, revised in 1920. I learned about a proper lady's weekly "at home" day when friends could call between 2:00 and 4:00 p.m. and remain for no more than twenty minutes—half an hour at most. I also learned about "visiting lists," with the names of people who frequently call during at-home days.

Since the pandemic struck, our visiting list has been empty, but we've had months of at-home days to clean up our stuff. Having hosted a couple of garage-sale fundraisers, we dread the prospect of another one. While greeting the neighbors is fun, setting up displays, pricing, and checking the change box is a nightmare. Even worse, professionals knock on the door at 6:45 a.m. seeking a preview. The aftermath is even worse. Somebody must clean up and haul away the unsold goods. That can cost money.

That's why we've been donating items slowly through Freecycle, Trash Nothing, and Next Door. You'd be surprised what you can get rid of when it's free, like wrapping paper remnants, posters, and cheap vases. However, the pricier stuff is a problem. Our children aren't interested in silver pedestal dishes or crystal bowls, and they fetch rock-bottom prices on eBay.

Marie Kondo offers a routine for clearing out stuff: start with clothing. But just as I was about to dispatch my favorite things, I encountered a snafu: because of the pandemic, Goodwill's GW Boutique in Menlo Park—which is so high-end that it provides shoppers with black-and-white cloth bags—was not accepting donations at the time. That's why I wound up at the Junior League's posh resale emporium, where donations were by appointment only. At 2:00 p.m. on a Tuesday, I parked my car behind the shop. In my trunk, I had laid out the clothing I thought was too good for Goodwill: A wine-colored Versace suit I wore at my 1998 bat mitzvah. My ivory wedding dress from 2000. An array of silk blouses and wool blazers. My mother's ermine jacket that I wore at a Purim party. Three volunteers spent five minutes rifling through my garments, and they nixed every single one.

"Too dated," they said, with apologies.

Once, I might have been rejected by the Junior League because I was Jewish. Fortunately, they don't do that anymore, but they can reject my favorite discards. Dejected, I packed everything into black lawn bags and drove to a nonjudgmental Goodwill.

Sorting through clothes is the easy part. But when it comes to Sentimental Objects I Can't Bear to Part With, I'm not much better than my late friend's mother. In my attic, I have four cartons of my newspaper clippings dating back to the 1960s. Two years ago, I put the best ones in a box labeled "to be scanned," but I didn't get around to the task. Some day.

With no emotional attachment, it was easy to filter through items in my friend's mother's house, discarding the junk and setting aside the good stuff for an estate sale. But my own history, nestled in attic boxes, is another proposition. Can I hold on to the memories while relinquishing the objects? I'm working on it.

CHAPTER 36

IT'S PROBABLY NOTHING[*]

2014

"It's probably nothing," the doctor said on my voicemail.

Those are three words one never wants to hear, particularly after a mammogram. If it were nothing, why would the doctor phone? In the past, she sent a brief note, using the self-addressed envelope I left at the lab.

I knew it was not "nothing." When I looked at the image of my left breast with the mammogram technician, everything looked clear. But on the side view of the right breast, I saw something suspicious, like a button. When I asked if it was the nipple, the technician said no.

"The radiologist will look at it," she said. "You'll probably hear in the middle of next week, since Monday's a holiday and we're closed."

I tried not to think about it, concentrating on my work: writing obituaries

---

[*] An earlier version of this chapter ran May 30, 2014, in *J. The Jewish News of Northern California*.

for the "In Memoriam" section of my fiftieth reunion directory for Oberlin. Nearly everybody had a story.

Bill, the class president whom we all adored, died of AIDS in 2001.

Liz, a children's software developer, died of complications of leukemia in 2003.

John had traveled to Vermont because his mother was ailing. The day after her death, he was murdered in a hotel room. He was forty-nine.

Martha, who married on graduation day, became a nurse practitioner. After her husband left, she entered seminary, becoming an Episcopal priest at age fifty-seven. Eight years later, she died of lymphoma.

When is my time? Will I be next? What will someone write about me?

Then I saw the red dot on my cell phone. A voicemail from Anonymous. My doctor had left a worrisome message telling me not to worry. However, I needed to come in for a more intensive mammogram and an ultrasound.

"It's probably nothing," I repeated, trying to reassure my husband. My friend Mary told my friend Judy, who sent me a "Thinking of you" email. I send those to people with incurable illnesses.

Was it time to plot the rest of my life? So many unwritten books, so much unfinished business. What should I be doing right now?

I made the follow-up appointment. The earliest I could be seen was the following week. Another week of brooding while trying not to brood. I had lived longer than the classmates I was writing about. Nora Ephron, whom I had interviewed in 2010, died two years later at age seventy-one. She had a whole folder labeled "Exit," devoted to her final plans. Should I have a folder? Would I lose my breast? My hair? Would the women in my synagogue's Caring Committee send over soup? Who would hold my hand when I expired?

I thought about the words delivered at so many Jewish funerals: "Life is a journey and death a destination." They did not cheer me up. I wanted to pray, but Judaism teaches that we're not allowed to pray for a result that has already been determined, so I prayed for strength and took long walks.

Returning to the mammogram room, I put on the flimsy gown once again, dropping one sleeve as the technician squished my right breast into a vise. I yelped. Then I held my breath. After the first three pictures, she took the images to the radiologist before completing all twenty pictures. Twenty ways to be squeezed senseless.

Shivering, I slipped my windbreaker over the gown and waited.

The technician returned. "The radiologist says she has all the X-ray information she needs," the technician said, "but she wants you to have the ultrasound."

I was led to another room where I lay on a table. The technician put a cold gel on my right breast. She took the images. Then she walked out. I waited again.

In the radiologist's office, I saw the images. It was all a blur to me.

"This looks like fibroadenoma," the radiologist said, pointing to a shadow. "It's like a fibroid, but it's in the breast. Based on my experience, I would say it's not cancer. But to be on the safe side, we need to keep an eye on it. You need to come back in six months for another mammogram and ultrasound."

A reprieve.

I drove home and made soup. For me.

CHAPTER 37

'I DON'T HAVE TIME FOR THIS'

2017

When you marry at twenty-two, as I did in 1965, you embark on a journey together believing your whole lives lie ahead. When you remarry at fifty-seven and sixty-two, as we did, you know that forever is illusive, particularly after heartbreaks, less-than-fulfilling relationships, and stretches of aloneness. If you open your eyes, you know your good time together could be short, but you push those thoughts aside, determined to enjoy what you have, here and now.

Then suddenly, reality intrudes, in the car, on a hike in Thailand's Hellfire Pass, or at a dress rehearsal.

On October 4, 2017, while dodging rush-hour traffic on the way to a charity dinner at the Computer History Museum, Allen received a call that reverberated over the dashboard. It was our family doctor. She had run tests. A "fishing expedition," she called it. Now she had results, and Allen had not one but two possibly life-threatening conditions.

A couple of months earlier, we received a premonition that our lives were about to change, but we shrugged it off. Allen was in perfect health. He looked far younger than his seventy-nine years, and he had more energy than I did. He worked out three times a week, enjoyed weekly bicycle rides with the Elder Spokesmen, fixed everything that was broken, and still managed to consult, sing solos in a couple of choirs, and take a class in memoir writing.

Allen is not a complainer, but while we were on a Baltic cruise that past July, he suddenly discovered that alcohol didn't sit well with him. We shrugged it off. Then on August 12, after a family lunch at a Mexican restaurant, we stopped on the way home in the historic town of Niles, filled with stores featuring Wild West memorabilia. While walking down the main street, Allen complained that he wasn't feeling well, so he found a bench and sat down while I browsed in a gourmet shop, purchasing Meyer lemon olive oil and strawberry-infused vinegar. Two days later, Allen awoke with a fever. He suspected pneumonia, so he called our family doctor. It wasn't pneumonia. It was something else, to be determined. The infection was possibly viral, probably idiopathic, the doctor said. "Idiopathic" means "cause unknown," or as one nurse friend says, GOK, God only knows. That said, our doctor suspected a heart problem.

Amid Allen's issues, I was grappling with my own. The breast lump *was* probably nothing, but I had IBS and acid reflux, which I thought were relatively minor. For some time, I couldn't drink most wines. Instead of dropping acid, I was bringing it up. Chocolate, which played havoc with my intestines, was also chancy, and partaking of wine and chocolate in the same meal brought on a headache. None of these problems seemed insurmountable, but our family doctor suggested I see a gastroenterologist, who scheduled a colonoscopy and an endoscopy. The colonoscopy results were only moderately troubling, but the endoscopy results surprised both the gastroenterologist and me. My illness had a label, Barrett's esophagus. In fine print, the illness had another label: precancerous. I was at risk of developing esophageal cancer, a horrendous illness. Would the illness impact my singing, my diet, my speech? Would I have to undergo radiation or surgery? Would it kill me?

I had watched my ex's mother, a lifelong smoker and nightly drinker, grapple with esophageal cancer for four years. She lost her taste buds as the result of radiation, and she also lost her will to live. She wouldn't even consider traveling to see her grandchildren, so we made the visits. We were there when she died, a few days after her sixty-fourth birthday.

For now, I could eat and I could sing, but I had to change my diet. No more wine, caffeinated coffee, beer, orange juice. No more hot and sour soup or high-acidity foods. I doubled my daily dose of omeprazole, an antacid, to forty milligrams. To counter the worsening of my osteoporosis, and more lost inches, I increased my calcium and weight-bearing exercises. I brewed half-caf coffee, which I poured into a breakfast cup filled with warm milk. To a coffeeholic, it was far from satisfactory, but when the alternative means death, you adjust.

Meanwhile, Allen's problems became increasingly frightening. His abdomen bloated, and he developed elephant ankles, unexplained swelling that made it impossible for him to wear most of his shoes. He saw a cardiologist, a pulmonologist who recommended a cardiology specialist at Stanford Hospital, and a hepatologist. He had more tests. He clearly had a serious condition, but no definitive diagnosis. Like me, he was told to eschew alcohol. Our barely drunk stash of single malt scotch, Irish whiskey, and vintage wines continued to gather dust.

Then came the phone call in the car. The "fishing expedition"—embarked upon to find the cause of Allen's idiopathic infection—revealed something completely unrelated: it was his prostate.

Many doctors stop testing for PSA—prostate-specific antigen—on men past age seventy. The theory is that they are more likely to die *with* prostate cancer rather than *of* it. Allen had no symptoms of prostate problems, nothing that showed up on annual physicals. His previous PSA test nine years earlier was within the normal range. But at seventy-nine, his PSA had soared to forty-three. The normal range for his age was 6.5 or less.

"We don't know if *the cancer*"—the doctor uttered the C-word—"has spread."

Allen and I looked at one another. Since he was driving, I jotted down the next steps, including the name of a urologic oncologist at Stanford.

We arrived at the dinner, where a good friend was being honored. She must have detected something in our countenances because she asked if everything was okay. We shrugged and said we would talk later in the week.

Many laters ensued. More tests, more appointments, more doctors, more diagnoses. In addition to a heart problem, Allen had prostate cancer, and we canceled a trip to India slated for January 2018. Instead, upcoming trips would be back and forth to clinics at Stanford Hospital. Allen underwent more testing, five weeks of daily radiation, and two years' worth of female hormone shots. Kiss conventional sex goodbye.

But the prostate cancer, easily treatable at this stage, had nothing to do with Allen's more alarming symptoms, and it wasn't his lungs, as he had suspected. The second cardiologist, a Stanford professor who took on only the most challenging patients, walked over to a screen and showed us the electrocardiogram of Allen's beating heart.

"Constrictive pericarditis," he said, inflammation of the saclike covering of the heart, cause unknown. Anti-inflammatory drugs brought Allen's elephant ankles back to semi-normal, so he could wear his shoes again. Diuretics lowered his weight, but his abdomen remained bloated, and his pants didn't fit. But the diuretics interfered with his sleep as they kept him hobbling to and from the bathroom. In addition, they sometimes lowered his normally low blood pressure to dangerous levels. More than once in the middle of the night, he fell in the hallway after getting up to urinate. When this happened, I would reach for the blood pressure monitor and fetch water. One night, his blood pressure registered 83 over 58, similar to my father's in the last hour of his life. Allen sipped water, took a potassium pill, and sat in a chair until he felt it was safe to return to bed. In the morning, we called the cardiologist.

"I don't have time for this!" Allen said, weeping after one too many trips to the clinics.

Neither do I, I thought to myself. *Neither do I.*

But time is what we have, so we keep going.

CHAPTER 38

WE ARE IN TRANSITION

2018

*O*ur financial adviser told us about the three stages of retirement: go-go, slow-go, and no-go. We are now in transition, but I'm not sure what the stage is, or when it leaves town.

The constrictive pericarditis, which is sometimes curable, did not go away. It's changed Allen's life, with medications adjusted daily. Every morning, he texts his cardiologist with his weight, blood pressure, and pulse rate. Then they decide whether he should up the dosage of one pill, eliminate another, or wait and see.

Three months after his diagnoses, we were scheduled to go to India with Overseas Adventure Travel. Since that would have delayed his cancer treatment, we diverted our deposit toward a December 2018 trip to Thailand. But before Thailand came a spring trip to the Galapagos and Machu Picchu. A day or two before we left, Allen collapsed in the hallway in the middle of the night. His blood pressure was alarmingly low. We checked with his cardiologist and decided to proceed with the trip. Fortunately, everything went well. Even while climbing at Machu Picchu and enduring the altitude at Cusco, we experienced no problems. Fortunately, I had taken a course of altitude sickness pills, which made all the difference.

Over the course of the next months, with the help of our medications, our health seemed to stabilize. I no longer awoke in the middle of the night with excruciating heartburn, or to the sound of Allen crashing in the hall on the way back from the bathroom. With those positive changes, we went ahead with our trip to Thailand. We have many happy memories. Every evening at our hotels, Allen would join the lounge singer, and he often soloed on such favorites as "My Way" and "Annie's Song." Sometimes I joined in.

We particularly enjoyed visits to traditional Thai villages, watching weavers and others practicing traditional crafts. During boat rides through the jungles, Allen would nosh on weird delectables, from fried rat to tiny raw shrimp just pulled from the river. Although I was horrified, Allen just laughed. His culinary proclivities became a running joke that, fortunately, didn't cause a case of the runs.

However, traversing the Hellfire Pass marked the beginning of slower go—not for me but for Allen. At this border region during World War II, some hundred thousand Allied forced laborers and Asians died under unspeakable conditions while building a railway for the Japanese. Today the site is a trail of tears, with crosses carved into rocks and long wooden staircases along the route, ending in a museum. While I was hiking ahead of Allen, one of the men in the group caught up with me, letting me know that Allen was flagging well behind the rest of the group. Allen was able to continue, at his own pace, but he let me know how difficult it was for him. Just six months before, Allen and I had climbed Machu Picchu, and while we didn't climb all the way to the summit, he didn't complain—although the broken steps and ruts were an obstacle. We had even climbed for a second day.

But Thailand, with its heat and humidity even in December, posed a more serious challenge. Either that, or Allen's condition had worsened. We arrived home December 19 after two flights and a fifteen-hour time difference. Caught up in holiday activities, I soon returned to a semi-normal sleep schedule. Allen did not. He was napping several times a day, including after breakfast and after dinner, and was barely able to work. A blood panel revealed that his sodium count was alarmingly low.

"Eat Chinese food," Dr. David said.

On the night of December 30, 2018, I was getting the house ready for our annual New Year's Eve party. We had been hosting this party for a good fifteen years, and every year it grew a bit bigger as friends and choristers joined us in a sing-along that I dubbed "the party of the year." I used to say it was one of the easiest events we hosted as we hired a pianist and a kitchen helper. Since we began the festivities after 9:00 p.m., we did not serve dinner or do much in the way of food preparation. Instead, we stocked the refrigerator with hors d'oeuvres from Costco and Trader Joe's and invited guests to bring finger foods or champagne. I always closed the invitations with a caveat: "Whatever you bring, you must take home, whether it's your dip or your date. We don't want to look at either of them in the morning."

Since Allen was still fatigued from the trip, we enlisted his daughters' help clearing all the furniture from the living room to provide room for our guests, which have numbered close to a hundred over the years. The night before the party, I needed Allen's help blowing up balloons and mounting them around the ceiling. Not exactly a challenging job.

"Okay," he said, "but I need a short nap. I'll be with you in half an hour."

That nap lasted most of the night. The naps continued, on and off, the next day, and even during the New Year's Eve party, when Allen absented himself a couple of times to lie down. I was certainly concerned about Allen, but I must admit I was also concerned about me, since the burden of the event had fallen on my shoulders. Even with help—and we had friends and relatives assisting with serving and cleanup, as well as a professional kitchen helper—I was wiped out. Later, I told Allen I could not stage another such event. He wasn't happy, but I was done. So was Allen, although he couldn't admit it then.

Meanwhile, the naps continued. Allen had another blood test. Then another. His sodium levels were so low that a doctor from Stanford Hospital phoned us, saying that Allen should go to the emergency room ASAP. Fortunately, our own doctors thought we could handle the problem at home. He was told he had been drinking too much water, which had diluted his sodium. Now in addition to eating Chinese food, he needed to curtail his water intake and instead drink V-8 juice, Gatorade, and other beverages that would help to balance his electrolytes. Before this, neither of us knew about the dangers of drinking too much water, unless it's done so on a dare, and we didn't have a clue about the importance of balancing electrolytes.

We canceled a planned river cruise to Vietnam and Cambodia—Allen was in no condition to tackle the Mekong River, Angkor Wat, or the Hanoi Hilton—and managed to receive a full refund, thanks to travelers' insurance and doctors' notes. That insurance was a godsend. At the time we were scheduled to be in Vietnam, Allen spent three days in Stanford Hospital for an undiagnosed gastrointestinal illness that may have been triggered by medications.

Instead of taking a summer trip, we rented a condo on the Capitola coast about an hour from home. We took walks along the beach to the Ghost Ship at Aptos, enjoyed lobster night at Zelda's on the Beach, read novels, and decompressed. I had planned to do some writing, which didn't happen, and I tried to forgive myself for vegging out. I also took on a couple of book-editing projects, one on stones and crystals, the other on feeling good. Editing other people's books helped me to get out of myself, assuaging the guilt about not getting on with my own writing.

Meanwhile, we were both out of shape, even though we were walking regularly and were exercising at the gym. Although Allen was not gaining weight, he had developed a pooch around the middle, something he had never had before, and I, too, had a bit of a pooch. I also was heavier than I had been in my ninth month of pregnancy.

In T. S. Eliot's "The Love Song of J. Alfred Prufrock," I recalled the words, "I grow old . . . I grow old . . . / I shall wear the bottoms of my trousers rolled." I am shrinking. When I last checked, I wasn't quite five feet tall. How could that happen?

I grow tired as I grow old. The holiday dinners for as many as twenty people used to seem easier. Now preparing a meal for fourteen people wipes me out. Before Thanksgiving, I told Allen I was not willing to host meals that required moving couches. I was grateful when my stepdaughter stepped up to the plate. We are passing the mantle.

In addition, my hearing has deteriorated. My brother shamed me into getting hearing aids. But he couldn't make me wear them. When I was running out to the gym, Allen asked me to stop at the drugstore and pick up his prescription. Then he called down to me from his upstairs office, asking if I could pick up a package of pens. Or so I heard.

Do we need pens? I wondered. Nonetheless, I returned with the prescription and a package of six black fine-point gel pens. I showed them to him. He looked quizzical.

"Those are nice, but do we need more pens?" he asked.

"Didn't you ask me to pick up a package of pens? That's why I bought them."

"Pens? I asked for a package of Depends."

We both burst out laughing.

CHAPTER 39

SOMETIMES IT IS A DRESS REHEARSAL

2019

*I*n the summer of 2019, the Assou Lezert chorale from Albi was arriving in Palo Alto again. We had been rehearsing for months, and we were more than ready. On the homefront, the house was clean, and Bolognese sauce and my Moroccan apricot chicken were in the freezer, awaiting our French houseguests. As we left for dress rehearsal at the church in Portola Valley, all the props for the concert were in the car.

I was the costume coordinator, and when we pulled into the parking lot, I dashed into the church carrying cowboy gear and several dozen sailor hats. What I had not noticed was that Allen hadn't followed me into the church. But others had. Just as we were about to go onstage, Susan, an alto, rushed over to me, shaking her head.

"Something's wrong with Allen," she said. "He's outside the church, on a bench."

On a bench?

Allen had collapsed in the parking lot, barely averting a fall.

I ran out of the church just as a bass and a baritone led Allen into a pew in the back. His color was gone. Dick, a physician, took Allen's pulse and shook his head. Fortunately, Allen has a direct line to his cardiologist on his cell phone. Dr. David would meet us at the hospital. Allen made it into the car with help from fellow choir members. His pulse was in the danger zone. His blood pressure measured sixty over forty, we found out later. And he was dizzy.

Months later, Allen told me he almost died July 9, 2019, the night of the dress rehearsal. At the time, all I knew was that I needed to drive down a dark country road to the hospital, and I loathe night driving. My heart pounded, yet he was the one with the heart condition. For once, he didn't criticize my driving.

"I was more gone than not," Allen said in reflection. "I could feel my pulse rate go slower and slower and the world kept going dimmer. . . . I began to gray out. Sounds grew faint. I no longer had the control of my hands. I didn't seem to be able to control my legs either. . . . All I know was that I was on my way out. I don't know what brought me back. It wasn't in my hands. Did I meet God? No!"

We did not meet God that night. We met Allen's cardiologist, who gave him every test he could think of—EKG, echocardiogram, sonogram—and all were okay. Allen had a choice: spend the night in the ER or return home and undergo a complete blood workup in the morning. He chose the latter.

By morning, all his numbers were normal. No electrolyte imbalance. What happened? Most likely a virus, the cardiologist said. Ironically, it had been a virus that had likely caused his pericarditis in 2017. But we will never know. Nobody still knows, so we live with it.

"Life is a gift," Allen says. So is choral singing, which has carried us through challenging times, and now we know why. Singing is good for the heart.

Fortunately, Allen recovered in time for our performance with the French chorale, and our time together went off without a hitch. We performed in Napa and Portola Valley, took our houseguests to Angel Island, and hosted an intimate Shabbat meal at our home. For the first time, our French visitors witnessed our ceremonies over candles, challah, and wine, joined by two Jewish women from our own choir. Most of our visitors had little contact with Jews, as none are in their choir and few are in their region, so Shabbat provided another dimension to our cross-cultural experience. So did our music, and we joined together in "California Dreaming," "Quand on n'a que l'amour" ("If We Only Have Love"), "Happy Together," and "C'est si bon" ("It's So Good"). How good it was, despite differences, or maybe because of them.

As for Allen, he hasn't had a recurrence of the alarming episode the night of the dress rehearsal, and he hasn't returned to the hospital. Yes, life is a gift, but it is also fragile. At our wedding ceremony in 2000, I promised never to take Allen "for granite." While he has long been my rock, sometimes I must be the strong one.

PART IV

COVID CHANGES EVERYTHING

CHAPTER 40

CANCELLATIONS

Winter 2020

On February 28, 2020, two weeks before our departure, we received an email from our rabbi: "Important Change Regarding Trip to Greece and Israel." The third paragraph began: "After serious consideration, we have decided that it would not be responsible for the . . . trip to go forward at this point. Unfortunately, at this late date, it is unlikely that there will be any reimbursement."

That shock, which arrived on a Friday afternoon, was just the beginning. It was far from the end, not by a long shot. We phoned one another: "Did you hear? Did you hear?" We also phoned our travel agent, who hadn't heard. The next month, the travel office was forced to close. Everything closed.

This would have been the synagogue's final trip with Rabbi Janet Marder, our popular rabbi who was retiring, and our first to areas of Greece and Israel that we hadn't visited, including Thessaloniki and Israel's southern desert.Not knowing what lay ahead, I wrote the following:

Just in Case

Half-packed suitcase on wooden chair.
Guidebooks on nightstand.
I book a table in Tel Aviv, a day in Delphi,
place papers on vacation hold,
not foreseeing holiday
on permahold.
Open email, just in case.
Just in case becomes empty case.
Call United, restock closet, drawers,
clear calendar;
precious plans crumble.
Friends pronounce platitudes:
Better safe than sorry!
It coulda been worse.
Words, well-meaning,
can't dispel
tiers of dejection.

April 2020

My college reunion in May, canceled. My cousin's June wedding in New Hampshire, also canceled. In-person choir practices, theater, opera, symphony, birthday parties, outings, all canceled, along with the cancellation of my son's visit from England. While we at first expected things to return to normal in a matter of weeks, we slowly came to accept that normal might never return.

We downloaded Zoom so we could keep up contacts and appearances. Heck, we soon learned to dress for Zoom, topping our pajama bottoms with stunning shirts. In our Zoom choir rehearsals, we listened to the director's voice and silenced our own. Was it fun? Well, it was good to see our friends, make small talk, and listen to the music, but for me, it was not enjoyable.

To create a performance video, we each had to record ourselves separately, wince as we played back our recordings, and eventually dispatch our recordings to a techie who would engineer the separate voices into a choir. The final result: a screen with human boxes, à la *Brady Bunch*. Of course, we applauded the engineer's skill in making us sound like an ensemble. But the best I could say is that we were making the best of it. Regardless of the end product, singing solo into an iPhone does not feel like making music with a choir.

We continued to make the best of it, and we listened to the appalling news on the pandemic and the political front, hoping things would get better but not feeling particularly confident. In a class on Mussar, the study of Jewish ethics, I pondered the soul traits of patience, trust, enthusiasm, and equanimity, recognizing that I was falling short on several fronts.

"The key to practicing equanimity is radical acceptance of what is," according to my teacher Greg Marcus's American Mussar website, americanmussar.com:

"**Too Little Equanimity:** We are hysterical, reactive and get too high and too low.

"**Too Much Equanimity:** We become ambivalent or oblivious to the rest of the world."

I couldn't accept what is, but I didn't have the energy to fight it. The result was an acute case of the blahs. During the early years of the pandemic, I was sleeping more than usual, and probably also eating more than I should. Yes, I continued to write, but while I was driven to toss words onto a screen, being compelled to write was not always cathartic.

CHAPTER 41

SOLITUDE: THE BRIGHT SIDE OF THE LOCKDOWN?*

Spring 2020

As we stroll along the sidewalks, we do-si-do with runners, dog walkers, and passersby. They wave as they dart off our path. We share homemade challah, buttermilk scones and dahlia tubers with next-door neighbors, and they in turn share fresh-laid eggs from their five chickens, whose cackling makes us smile. Meanwhile, the neighbor on the other side asks for our shopping lists as he heads to the markets, and every time our tenant goes to Costco, he picks up an extra rotisserie chicken for us.

"It's my treat," he tells us. Later, he will leave me discarded chicken bones for the soup I make almost weekly.

Our planned choir performances at nursing homes and senior residences are not happening. Instead, we attend remote choir rehearsals on Zoom, where

---

* An earlier version of this chapter appeared June 23, 2020, in *J. The Jewish News of Northern California.*

time distortions preclude a harmonious blend, forcing us to silence ourselves while singing. We gladly greet one another's postage-stamp images, but we do not touch, do not hug, do not hear each other sing. On Friday nights, we chant the prayers as our rabbi and cantor lead us—via a laptop on the dining room table. But we don't invite our friends to Shabbat dinner.

Yet as our physical world has shrunk, and we rarely venture beyond walking distance, our eyes have opened wider to our immediate world, taking in sights we had barely noticed. The neighbors we once waved to perfunctorily as we pulled our car out of the driveway are now friends. Like pioneer families of old, we are in this adventure together, and we are interdependent. Will these relationships hold in better times? That remains to be seen.

As our streets have grown quieter, with fewer cars on the road and fewer planes in the air, we inhale the jasmine in the evening air and hear the birds. We take in the accidental tangle of red-violet sweet peas and lemon-yellow nasturtiums climbing on the side of the house, the redwood grove nearby, the chalk drawings on the sidewalk where kids play hopscotch, just as we once did.

In our unwanted staycation, the garden thrives, and we savor homegrown herbs and lettuces. With no place to go, the car rarely leaves the driveway, and everything moves more slowly. As horizons narrow, we discover a neighborhood and a homeland we always had and never knew.

CHAPTER 42

ALLEN SHACKS UP WITH TEDDY BEARS

Summer 2020

With nothing more severe than my usual springtime allergy symptoms, I drove to the Stanford campus for a PCR test. I wanted to reassure my husband and brother, who are both immunocompromised, that I didn't harbor the deadly coronavirus. If I was seeking reassurance, what transpired was something else. Here is the story:

Test No. 1

June 23, 2020. During the early days of the pandemic, self-administered antigen tests were not yet available for home use. That's why I drove into a mobile test facility on the Stanford campus. A masked, white-clad technician reached through my car window and stuck an oversized nasopharyngeal swab into my left nostril. On June 24, a nurse phoned. My test was faulty and had to be repeated.

Test No. 2

On June 26, I repeated the test, this time asking the tester to use the right nostril. It hurt like hell. The next day as I was preparing a casserole with left-over turkey, the phone rang. It was a nurse from Stanford. Seeking confirmation that she had reached the right person, she asked me my name and date of birth. The call, she said, was about my second PCR test.

Oh no! Would I have to take the test a third time? Could my nostrils tolerate another test?

I began chattering about the faulty June 23 test and asked her if they were able to get a reading from the second test.

"Yes," she said matter-of-factly.

Whew!

"It was positive!"

I don't remember if I went into shock immediately or later as I listened to the many precautions I would have to take: Self-isolate. Use a separate bath-room. Sleep in a separate bedroom. Eat in a separate area. Avoid contact with all others, including those in our household. Tell everybody you've been in contact with that they need to get tested as well.

I could see the disbelief on my brother's face as he stood frozen in the living room, hearing only my end of the phone conversation and trying to glean what was being said on the other end. While all three of us are in the vulnerable age group, I am the healthiest one. I am the one who does the cooking and most of the cleaning. I am the one who weeds the garden and picks the lettuce, herbs, and tomatoes for summertime dinners.

After I put the turkey casserole into the convection oven, I retired from culinary duties. For the next ten days, my husband and brother would take care of meals. My job was to get well—even though I wasn't sick.

Meanwhile, I dashed off an email to friends and family, telling them that I took a PCR test, even though I had no symptoms. I was one of the lucky asymptomatic cases. I could still smell the jasmine and the rosemary in the garden.

I could still taste Thai food. I hadn't lost my appetite.

However, we had to cancel a two-week vacation in a Capitola condo with a view of the ocean. Good friends with whom we had walked and lunched had to cancel a planned road trip to visit their son in Seattle. They were understandably miffed.

I was also angry at myself. I had been so careful. I wore a mask in public. For the first three and a half months of the shutdown, I barely left the house except to walk around the block. Neighbors had done most of our shopping. However, I had made a couple of masked forays to the grocery and drugstores, and after several months of sheltering in place, I had begun to ease up a bit, getting together in the backyards of friends and family.

Could I have picked up the virus from one of them? Could it have been the bananas I fingered at Trader Joe's? The paper towels at CVS? The newspaper at the end of the driveway? The six-pack of zinnias at the garden store? Did I fail to wash my hands sufficiently?

Could the test have been a false positive?

I sent a note to my doctor, who replied, "It is possible, but not very likely."

Fortunately, both my brother and my husband tested negative, but because of their exposure to me, they remained in semi-quarantine.

Several times a day, I would place my index finger into an oximeter to test my blood oxygen level. It was always above 95, which is normal. My temperature rarely rose above 97.5. I was a statistic, an asymptomatic Typhoid Mary, or Covid Cornelia, trying to stay healthy.

Test No. 3

At the suggestion of my doctor, I was tested again on July 1. My nostril felt abused, but I was still symptom-free. I could continue to edit and write. My husband and brother brought my meals to the dining room table while they ate in the kitchen. I had the use of our bedroom, the master bathroom, and my office. Allen moved into the teddy bear room, where visiting grandkids stay. My brother continued to sleep in the guestroom.

Shani, Allen's younger daughter, took our shopping list to Trader Joe's. She returned with so many frozen foods that we could barely close the small freezer above the fridge. Then she wouldn't accept a penny from us. It's wonderful to have such dear family members.

Feeling relatively okay, I put on a mask and took a mile walk around the neighborhood. The steam under my mask made me sweat. When I arrived home, my temperature was 99.3, which is high for me. Could the temperature rise have been caused by the mask? By 8:00 p.m., my temperature dropped to 98.1.

Everybody asked why I had bothered to be tested when I had no symptoms and no known exposure. In a nutshell, I thought it was a precaution. It wasn't a bother, or so I thought, before those oversized cotton swabs were stuck up my nostrils. Did I feel horrible because I unwittingly exposed others? Did I feel awful that friends and family had to be tested? Of course. But I couldn't do a rewind. So I waited for better results.

Congestion Sets In

On July 2, I awakened at 6:00 a.m. with a stuffy nose, and I gulped down water. I couldn't find a readable decongestant in the medicine chest, so I took a homeopathic pill with illegible Chinese print on which I had written: "For stuffy nose."

Well, that can't hurt, I told myself.

Just in case, I checked my email: If I had the virus, I would get a call from a nurse, but if I didn't have the virus, I would find a reassuring note from Stanford.

Fortunately, I found a reassuring note:

"SARS-CoV-2, the COVID-19 virus, was NOT detected in your nasopharyngeal sample."

What? My nose was all stuffed up, but I am not gonna die: no hospital, no ventilator, go figure.

I awakened my husband in the teddy bear room. I shouted to my brother in the guestroom. They cheered. I cheered.

Allen was now singing. He got ready to return to our bedroom. "No more teddy bears," he said. "They'll miss me."

But it wasn't the end at all.

Note to my doctor re: test results question

So, was this all a bad dream? No COVID-19, but now I have a stuffy nose. Meanwhile, many of my friends were tested, and one couple canceled a vacation. I guess I was one of the false positives. If I had "gotten better" this quickly, I wouldn't be congested. Go figure.

Note from my doctor re: test results question

Hi Janet: It's hard to know what's going on. Was the first test a false positive, or the second test a false negative? Let's recheck you in about five days. If you're negative again, I'd go with the former. I will place the order now.

New note to my doctor re: test results question

Thanks. In five days, my nose should have recuperated:).

Bottom line: Allen was back with the teddy bears.

Teddy Bears' Picnic Is No Picnic

On July Fourth, we did not barbecue. We did not get together with friends or family. We did not watch fireworks. Instead, I masked the teddy bears, who joined my masked husband and brother for a virtual picnic in the backyard. I placed the Teddy Bears' Picnic photo on my Facebook page to provide friends a moment of levity. But it was no laughing matter for us. My husband and brother remained semi-quarantined, and I remained in isolation. With nothing more serious than sinusitis, I could work, editing a travel book with incredible photos of coastlines all over the world. With no distractions, I finished the project well before the deadline. As I've said before, my epitaph will read, "She always made deadline." But I was not ready to check out. Not anytime soon.

Earlier that day, at the end of my synagogue's virtual Saturday morning Torah study, I told fellow congregants what my family was going through, warning them about the importance of sheltering in place, social distancing, and mask wearing. Even though I had no fever, no cough, and no COVID-19 symptoms, I still did not know if I harbored the virus, had an asymptomatic case, or had been previously infected. The jury was out until I tested negative a second time, so I remained in isolation.

The night of the Fourth, my husband walked in to say good night, socially distancing at the other side of the room. He said he missed me. We could not hug. We could not touch. He was sentenced to at least four more nights with the teddy bears. We both looked at one another, shaking our heads, trying to hold back tears.

In three more days, I would receive my fourth test for COVID-19. But until a second negative test, I remained in limbo, along with my husband and brother.

Test No. 4

On July 7, I drove to the testing facility and endured nasal abuse again. Once again, I returned home and waited on pins and needles for results. That night, I awakened at midnight. I awakened again at 2:00 a.m. I awakened again at 3:40 a.m. after a bad dream in which my husband fell in love with a young French woman during a trip to Paris and decided to leave me. Then I checked my email for a note from Stanford. *Nada.* No news is not good news.

After four tests for COVID-19, I knew the drill: If the results were good, I would probably receive an email in the wee hours of the morning. If the news were dire, a nurse would call later in the day to deliver the grim verdict.

I awakened again at 5:00 a.m. with a stuffy nose and a bad case of anxiety.

I made tea, the universal cure, filled a bowl with blueberries, and sat down to read the news on my iPad. No good news. Not in the world. Not at home. Not in my email. At 5:30 a.m., I went outside to pick up the newspaper. The air felt good, the news did not, and my agitation continued.

Here we go again! More isolation? What will be next?

Okay, I finally said to myself. I'm not going to die, at least not of COVID-19. What could I do to ease my anxiety? I watered the seedlings I was nurturing on the patio. I inspected the wild arugula, growing well in small pots. I looked at the teeny Chief Red Flame celosias I had planted from seeds. The tomatoes in the vegetable garden were turning reddish. Red is a good color.

Then I grew drowsy—a good sign—and I hopped into bed again, awakening an hour later at 6:40 a.m. I opened my email and found a new message from Stanford:

"SARS-CoV-2, the COVID-19 virus, was NOT detected in your nasopharyngeal sample."

I did not read the long list of symptoms and precautions. Instead, I freshened up and made my way to the teddy bear room to awaken my husband.

"Any news?" he asked.

I smiled and gave him a hug.

When I relayed my dream, he smiled. He wasn't going to France. He was going back to our bedroom.

Postnasal Script

Later, I tried to get answers from Stanford Medicine. How could this have happened? Could my testing sample have been switched with someone else's? How rare is a false positive test such as my own? A few weeks later, I received a note from a pathology professor that false positives from Stanford's testing accounted for 0.1 percent. When I met with my own doctor, she shook her head and said, "It's more than that."

Meanwhile, we placed a masked teddy bear on the park bench on our porch, a message to the neighborhood. As the chief said on *Hill Street Blues*, "Let's be careful out there."

CHAPTER 43

AMID A PANDEMIC, BLOND IS SO YESTERDAY*

December 2020

Our back lawn is sprouting clouds of gray, remnants of our COVID-19 haircuts safely executed outdoors. My husband had salt-and-pepper hair when he answered my 1999 ad in the *Jewish Bulletin*. Now the pepper is gone. I am running out of pepper, which has migrated to the back of my neck, invisibly. Full frontal, in the mirror, I am gray, and I see my mother. Now in my eighth decade, I have earned my gray locks. I will never go blond, like the older women in my mother's building. I will also never choose to go orange, lavender, or pink, although my hair has turned all those shades, much to my consternation.

In my forties, I had dyed my hair a couple of times, but after a month or two in the sun it had begun to turn orange. Even worse, the fumes from the dye

---

* An earlier version of this chapter appeared December 11, 2020, in *J. The Jewish News of Northern California*. Some information was in my column of November 25, 1990, in the *Oakland Tribune*.

made me gasp, so I left the salon while the color processed, standing in the alleyway where I was surrounded by stylists on a cigarette break. After that experience, I went the do-it-yourself route.

First, I tried Clairol Loving Care, a temporary rinse touted as covering only the gray. Ha! It covered everything but the gray—towels, shower tiles, and the sink. My wiry gray strands put up a valiant battle and resisted the assault with bravado. Not so the shower curtain at the Holiday Inn in San Diego.

After that episode, I called Clairol's hotline for advice. My problem, I was told, was Resistant Gray Hair. The expert recommended the stronger stuff, so I bought a bottle of Nice'n Easy, in a medium-warm-brown shade. At first it was nice and easy. Then it became hateful. After two months of oxidizing in the sun, my hair was turning auburn, with a line of demarcation at the roots. I was in danger of sabotaging my fuchsia lipstick, my wardrobe, and my integrity. Medium ash brown toned down the auburn and helped me through spring, but after I sat through *Richard III* on a hot day in Golden Gate Park, Agent Orange returned with a vengeance.

Once again, I called the Clairol hotline and was told to try Loving Care. Hadn't I done that once before? After I spent thirty-five dollars on a color-corrective product, the orange disappeared, and my days of dabbling in dyes and rinses ended—for an entire decade.

But in 2000, shortly after I remarried, my hairdresser persuaded me to try a new semi-permanent rinse that contained no peroxide or ammonia. After my husband said, "You look terrific," I was back on the bottle.

For the next twenty years, I experimented with shades of Clairol Beautiful, which I applied at home. It did not turn my hair orange. It did not turn my hair blue. And it did not make me gasp. But during the summer of 2019, I began receiving interesting comments about my punkish pinkish-lavender hair.

"It's really cute," my teenage granddaughter said. "I love it!"

But not everybody loved it. At an outdoor reception, a synagogue member drew me aside. "Janet, what *are* you putting on your hair these days?" she said.

"It's pink!"

"Hmm," I said. "I'm not putting anything new on my hair. I've been at the beach, and the sun must be having its way with me."

The next time I saw her, with my hair freshly rinsed in ashen brown, she said, "Much better. Now you look like *you* again."

Then COVID-19 came along, and I went off the bottle. I trashed the silvery Advanced Gray bottles recommended for super-resistant gray: They contained toluene, reputed to be carcinogenic. Then I tossed the non-toluene-containing copper-colored bottles: Honey Brown, Cedar-Red Brown, Medium Ash Brown, Medium Warm Brown. Gone, gone, gone.

After four months without a haircut during COVID-19 isolation, I phoned my hairdresser, who brought her tools to the backyard. Now semi-retired, she had stopped using hair coloring herself, but she wondered why I had decided to go gray.

I thought of the women in my mother's apartment building. They grew blonder and blonder as they aged. I thought of my mother, who finally embraced the gray, which was less aging than the blond of her friends and neighbors. I also thought of Glenn Close, Jane Fonda, Diane Keaton, Rita Moreno, and Helen Mirren.

"I'm starting to like my gray hair," I said. "Blond is so yesterday."

CHAPTER 44

THE YELLOW-BELLIED FLUFFERNUTTER AND THE BLUEBIRD OF PASSOVER*

Passover 2021

*O*nce again, we have foiled the Angel of Death, and the pandemic. Since we were fully vaccinated, we invited Allen's family to share an afternoon Passover seder on our patio.

Winter had passed. Tulips, daffodils, and snapdragons were abloom in our garden. We had not heard the voice of the turtle in our land, as if a turtle has much of a voice, but the birds were chirping merrily. Thanks to the feeder on our clothesline, we host myriad flying creatures whose names we don't know, so we make them up: yellow-bellied fluffernutter, cross-eyed bush thatcher, dapple-tailed window-splasher. But in the middle of our seder, we saw a huge

---

* An earlier version of this chapter appeared April 2, 2021, in *J. The Jewish News of Northern California.*

blue scrub jay, almost too big for the holes in the feeder. Allen's older daughter captured the moment on her cell phone. After we recited Passover blessings, for wine, matzah, and parsley (*karpas*), Spencer, our youngest grandson, asked if we have a blessing for bird seed.

"Of course," we chorused, making one up on the fly. "*Baruch Atah Adonai, Eloheinu Melech HaOlam, Borei Pri Ha* Bird Seed" (Blessed are you, our Lord our God, king of the universe, who creates bird seed).

The adults responded with an "Amen," and we laughed, recognizing that the children have taught us a new lesson about gratitude.

In a traditional seder, the children ask the Four Questions in the Haggadah. The first: "Why is this night different from all other nights?" In 2021, we added a new question: "Why is this Passover different from all other Passovers?"

In 2019, two years before, we sat at tables that filled the living room, surrounded by twenty people in our extended family. In 2020, my husband, brother, and I sat around a leafless table, and we shared our ceremony with extended family via Zoom.

In 2021, our Sunday seder was outdoors in the afternoon, another first. We talked about freedom from oppression and pharaohs. Ryan wanted to know if the bad guy in the Haggadah is Ramses I, II, or III. We had no idea. But since the name of the biblical pharaoh is unimportant, we began to talk about modern-day pharaohs, leaders who oppress their nations. For Ryan, the first name that came to his mind was that of a former president whose name we will not utter. Ryan didn't hesitate to voice his discontent with that guy, expressing gratitude that America has a new leader.

We also talked about plagues, then and now—hunger, racism, sexism, injustice, climate change—and we continued to express gratitude. Allen's daughters praised the meal, especially the matzah ball soup, which they look forward to every year. Spencer even tasted the gefilte fish, which his mother, aunt, and brother won't touch. His tasting called for a *Shehechiyanu*, the blessing after something is done for the first time, or after a long time. That was the case with the seder itself. We had come through. Perhaps the masks would come off soon. But we could still see smiles in one another's eyes.

We have passed through difficult times, and more may lie ahead, but on Passover we can still give back as we feed family, share ancient traditions, and create new ones. Just as Elijah appears every year at our unorthodox seders, when Allen retreats from the room and returns as a biblical prophet with a rag mop on his head and a wineglass in his hand, maybe next year a bluebird will grace our seder again. If not, we will recall how she once blessed us with her presence.

CHAPTER 45

PANDEMIC SHABBATS–AND LESSONS TO CARRY FORWARD[*]

March 2021

*I*t's Friday evening. The fragrance of cooked turkey breast with rosemary and roasted garlic potatoes fills the house. The dining room table is festively set with red linens, flowers from the garden, Portuguese candlesticks, a pewter wine cup, a cloth-covered homemade challah—and an incongruous laptop.

We light the candles, bless the wine, and chant the bread blessing. As we follow the service on our computer, we nosh our way through another Zoom Shabbat: dining, praying, harmonizing. For more than a year, my husband, brother, and I have honored Shabbat at our dining room table, transformed into a makeshift sanctuary each weekend with our new routines: services via Zoom followed by informal breakout sessions with friends who used to dine out together after synagogue services.

---

[*] An earlier version of this chapter appeared April 16, 2021, in *J. The Jewish News of Northern California*.

On Saturday morning, our weekly Torah study follows a similar course. Instead of bagels at the synagogue, we sip our coffee as we peruse the parashah (weekly Torah portion), raising electronic hands to share thoughts on Zoom. After, we break into small groups to discuss the Torah or just schmooze.

We've had our vaccination shots, and soon we hope to greet our friends inside the synagogue or in the outdoor chapel. We will socialize during pre-prayer snacks, harmonize during the service, and dine with friends afterward. We imagine going to a favorite eatery and eating inside, rather than ordering takeout, which inevitably loses something in transport, like the crispy Chinese noodles that are soft and squishy by the time they arrive home.

Soon we hope to retire what we call our "Zoomies"—tops with anything-goes bottoms, such as sweats, workout leggings, or jammies. Once again, we will look in the mirror before we leave the house and check our head-to-toe silhouettes, putting on real shoes instead of slippers.

I look forward to in-person encounters with friends and clergy we have seen only on-screen. Eventually, we may even hug or shake hands instead of elbow bumping. And I dearly look forward to being a dinner guest or attending a potluck.

That said, how will we handle a serve-yourself supper? Will our houses of worship follow the example of the cruise lines, stationing gloved, masked servers at the buffet tables?

During the pandemic, we have been fortunate that my husband's daughters and grandchildren live nearby, so we have been able to share backyard birthday parties and masked encounters in our driveways. In addition, we have not experienced the boredom or the isolation that have beset so many. Even though we are nominally retired, we continue to take on professional projects. And we have not faced the financial hardships of those whose unemployment is not by choice.

When this global nightmare dissipates, we look forward to attending theater and concerts, singing with our choirs, and sitting around a table with classmates in our writing workshops.

But one thing we don't look forward to is the stress of leaving the house before seven in the evening to attend meetings and rehearsals, barely allowing enough time to hunt for a parking place. In the year since March 2020, I don't think I put gas in the Prius more than a half-dozen times. Inevitably, I'll be spending more money on gas, and more time on the road.

What have I learned from this unplanned staycation? I've learned that I'm overprogrammed and overscheduled, and I don't take enough time to just sit in nature and do nothing. There's something to be said for the flipside of John Dewey's "learning by doing" philosophy. How about learning by *not* doing, or by just being?

For me as a writer and for my husband as an inventor, inspirations come to us when we let our minds travel while our bodies are still. In the last year, by staying in and dining at home, we have learned to take things more slowly, particularly enjoying the tranquility of Shabbat.

In "The World Is Too Much with Us," Wordsworth laments that "Getting and spending, we lay waste our powers; [. . .] We have given our hearts away."

As we go forward, can we manage to retain some of this quietude as our worlds open again?

CHAPTER 46

A TAXING TRIFECTA

The Little People

Upstairs, the Little People, tiny dolls of her childhood,

lie in boxes in the playroom:

Downstairs, blanketed in pink, she lies on the sofa.

Blond strands that are not hers

tumble across a pillow,

As daughter naps,

Mom picks up her book, reads a bit, watches.

Like the set-aside Little People

of a long-ago life,

she waits for a cue.

2021

When we had finally accustomed ourselves to the new normal, a taxing trifecta struck our family. First, we learned that my ex-husband had Alzheimer's, a situation that disrupted the lives of my two grown children: my daughter in Southern California, my son in the north of England. Then on Saturday, February 6, 2021, my daughter sent a troubling email headlined "Sad News." Her husband had lost his father over the summer. *Who else, God? Who else?*

"I have some really bad news that I just found out about yesterday. I thought about calling you all, but just couldn't bring myself to listen to all of your reactions, which I knew would be too hard for me to see and hear," she wrote.

"Sit down before you read this! I have invasive carcinoma breast cancer that has metastasized and spread to my lymph nodes. . . .

"P.S. Emailing me back is much safer if you would like to do that, as then you don't have to worry that I will see your sadness. . . . "

I forwarded her email to my husband and to my brother. Letting the news sink in, I told them I didn't want to talk. Not yet.

What could I do? I took a deep breath and replied to my daughter, "How can I help?" Visiting was out of the question. We hadn't yet had our Covid shots, and I couldn't hop on an airplane.

My daughter talked. I listened. Then months of chemo started. We emailed, texted, and shared favorite Psalms and songs, compatible with both her Christianity and my Judaism. She was particularly touched when I sent her my favorite Psalm, number 121: "I look to the hills . . . " I also phoned Peg Krome, my friend and spiritual director, who sang "Healer of the Broken-Hearted" with me, based on Psalm 147. Later my own choir, HaShirim, sang "Heal Us Now," dedicating the song to my daughter as she watched via Zoom. While she could see us, she could not hear us, as our voices were muted as we sang in our Zoom squares to a recording. Nonetheless, she was touched that we were sending prayers her way.

By early April, after Passover and Easter, I was two weeks past my second

Covid shot and could finally fly to San Diego to see my daughter. I transported soup bones and ingredients for chicken soup on the plane: Jewish penicillin. On a Tuesday morning, she and I took a walk along the ocean in La Jolla. Looking adorable, she concealed her baldness with a cute flip of blond hair attached to a baseball cap. Nobody could tell. But that evening, after returning from a round of chemo, she put a simple nightcap over her bald head and crashed on the sofa, cuddling her two dogs.

My daughter was fortunate to have the support of so many: Her fellow teachers at the school where she teaches kindergarten. The kids and their parents. Her church friends, who were providing meals and support. Her recently widowed mother-in-law. How could I help? What could I do?

The day before I left San Diego, I baked two loaves of challah: one for my daughter and her family, another to take home for Shabbat. I returned home on Friday, April 9, in good spirits, optimistic about my daughter's journey. She was doing beautifully. Then the following Monday morning, April 12, our lives took a turn for the worse.

My brother awoke in excruciating pain. "Call an ambulance," he said, in a raspy, barely audible voice. "There's no way I can get out of bed."

A fire truck and an ambulance pulled up. Eight EMT men came to the door. One of them met with me in the living room, taking notes about my brother's condition: his disabilities, his history, his insurance. The other seven descended upon my brother's room, lifted him into a hammock-like contraption, placed him on a gurney, and whisked him off to Stanford Hospital a couple of miles away. I was told there was no hurry. I could finish my breakfast, finish my coffee. But my husband could not accompany me to the hospital. With Covid restrictions, only one family member was allowed in the emergency room, so I had to leave alone.

Grabbing my water bottle, I drove off at 8:20 a.m. amid rush-hour traffic and spent the next eight hours in the ER. I couldn't leave the cubicle except to use the bathroom. I couldn't visit the cafeteria, which was closed to visitors during

Covid. I couldn't step outside. Not if I wanted to come back in. I had nothing to eat until around 4:00 p.m., when a kind nurse offered me a well-wrapped turkey sandwich and a box of cranberry juice.

Meanwhile, nurses and physicians came in and out of the cubicle, many wearing colorful caps and kerchiefs. We conferred with surgeons, gastroenterologists, others. X-rays, MRIs, and other tests proceeded. Second opinions. My brother had a bowel blockage. At first, the doctors and nurses tried to deal with the obstruction nonsurgically, but their attempts only intensified the pain. As my brother became sicker, the doctors decided on emergency surgery. Around 4:30 p.m. my brother was whisked upstairs to a lovely room with a view of the surrounding hills. Once again, I thought of Psalm 121 and looked to the hills for hope as my brother was conveyed to the operating room.

The surgery was a success, but the patient was not doing well. For the better part of two weeks, he was fed intravenously. When he was finally able to sit up and eat solid food, he was taken to a subacute facility in Palo Alto. When he arrived, he was able to use a walker and transfer from bed to chair to bathroom. Two weeks later, he could not. His weight dropped from 155 at the time of the surgery to 143 two weeks later. A month after the surgery, he weighed 139. Something was dreadfully wrong.

Unfortunately, my brother was admitted to a nursing home on a Saturday afternoon, when staffing was minimal and rehab virtually nonexistent. He was left unattended for several hours in the wrong kind of bed for a patient with a pressure wound. Pressure wounds (bedsores) are usually the result of hospital and nursing home negligence. Left to fester, an infected wound can become septic, ultimately causing organ failure and even death. Because of inattention at that time and on subsequent weekends—when doctors are rarely around to see that their orders are carried out — my brother developed a painful stage-four infection that kept him virtually bed-bound for the better part of two months. Vertigo complicated his recovery.

As my brother's next of kin and primary caregiver, I tried to keep on top of things because he couldn't. When my brother finally was discharged in mid-June, we told the staff that had my brother received proper treatment at the beginning of his stay, chances are he would have returned home after two or three weeks. The head nurse took our complaints to heart. But he was admitted on her day off.

An ailing patient, I said, requires just as much care on a Sunday as on a Monday. But the doctor's orders to turn my brother every two hours were not followed. Once, when my brother's call button went unanswered, I ran through the hallways to recruit a couple of attendants. On another weekend, we asked a nursing assistant to help my brother out of bed and were told nobody was available to lift him until Monday, when physical therapists were on hand. When my husband complained at the nursing station, a couple of attendants came to my brother's aid, but unfortunately, they could not lift him without causing pain. Perhaps that explains why, at one point, he went eleven days without a shower.

As I spoke with social workers, advocates, and former patients, I discovered that our nursing home system was in disrepair, with a shortage of beds and staffing, along with concerns about how state and federal funding is allocated.

Even before Covid, "the generally low quality of care and poor oversight of these nursing homes was well known," according to AARP California Director Nancy McPherson[*]: "Between 2006 and 2015, the number of substandard care deficiencies cited in nursing facilities increased by 31 percent." However, during the same period, "the net income for three of the largest nursing home companies in California increased significantly."

Friends who had been placed in posher facilities also complained about inadequate care. "On Mother's Day, they put flowers on the table, but I couldn't get a nursing assistant to answer my call button on a Saturday night," said a friend

---

[*] "Statement of AARP California State Director Nancy McPherson," *AARP*, (March 25, 2021), https://states.aarp.org/california/statement-of-aarp-california-state-director-nancy-mcpherson-on-the-protect-package-of-nursing-home-reform-bills

who recently was at an upscale facility in Santa Clara County.

"I could ring the bell a hundred times, and nobody would answer," said Carole, who had been placed in a modern South Bay facility. "If somebody doesn't have an advocate, they're really screwed."

CHAPTER 47

MOVING DISRUPTIONS

2021

On a Friday evening in May, we blessed the homemade challah and prepared to celebrate Shabbat. At 6:30 p.m., minutes after a peaceful Shabbat service began on Zoom, a seventy-foot truck transported a weekend from hell to our front door. Over the next five hours, almost until midnight, two men carried all my brother's furniture, books, paintings, carpets, and kitchen equipment to a storage room behind our garage. But my brother wasn't home. He was still in a subacute facility, the euphemism for a nursing home, a mile away.

When he came to stay with us in 2016, he had parked his household goods in a Long Island storage unit and moved into our front bedroom. Storing his possessions on Long Island, paying $145 a month, didn't make sense, so he finally bit the bullet and spent $4,000 to have them transported to our home. But they weren't supposed to arrive on a Friday night in the middle of dinner.

At first, we were told the truck would arrive between 2:00 and 4:00 p.m., then between 5:00 and 6:00 p.m. We weren't prepared to supervise the move in the dark. Nor were we prepared to deal with a truck the size of two mobile homes that straddled our street. Fortunately, our kind neighbors moved their cars to give the truck enough room.

The drivers were frustrated. Their earlier deliveries were in San Francisco, where they moved furniture from the truck to a vehicle that could negotiate city streets. That's why they were so late, and so apologetic. Normally, they would shower at a truck stop before sleeping in the truck. Feeling sorry for the movers, my husband invited them to use our shower. They thanked him profusely.

Before the move, we had cleared out a room off our garage. Now it was packed to the rafters, with dressers sitting on end and inverted chairs atop cartons that were piled to the ceiling. On the curb, the movers parked my brother's queen-size mattress, box spring, and wrought iron headboard, awaiting the twice-yearly extra-refuse removal the following Monday.

The next morning, I awakened laughing after a bizarre dream. A miniature horned goat, a hen, and two other small farm animals were cavorting in our kitchen skylight. In my dream, my husband watched the whole scene and smiled, beatifically. When I relayed the dream, he said things could have been worse. Thank God the rhinos and the elephants didn't show up.

We were fortunate that the citywide extra-trash cleanup came the Monday after the move. We had spent the week cleaning out our shed and garage, bringing unused skis, patio umbrellas, electronic equipment, and miscellaneous junk to the curb. The sanitation workers crushed everything in minutes.

When I ran to the curb, too late, half a mattress was in the jaws of the truck.

"You should have marked it 'Donations,'" we were told. But it probably wouldn't have made any difference. Other stuff, some marked, some not, was crushed indiscriminately.

My husband looked at me. "It's not ours anymore," he said. "Be glad that it's gone."

The rest of the furniture awaited my brother's recovery. So did we.

CHAPTER 48

IS OUR MARRIAGE AT STAKE?

2021

When my brother returned to our home after twelve days in the hospital and eight weeks in the nursing home, his care was more than we could handle. He fell twice the second day he was home. He could not get in and out of bed easily. He estimated that he spent twenty-one hours a day in bed for a couple of weeks. Three months after he arrived home, visiting nurses and physical and occupational therapists no longer visited, but his pressure wound required daily treatment, and I had become an irritable Nurse Nancy. Covid isolation and canceled vacations had exacerbated my moods.

"I want a whole wife, not half a wife," my husband asserted as we cleared the breakfast table. "Our living situation is deteriorating, and it will become even worse. We cannot care for your brother any longer. If he doesn't go, I will leave."

My stomach churned as his words sank in. The man I married in the year 2000, in what our friends regarded as a storybook marriage, did not make idle threats. And when mild-mannered Allen digs in his heels, he releases an ogre. Nobody can compromise with an ogre. Nobody can reason with an ogre. You can't kiss an ogre and expect him to turn into a prince. The ogre needs to be calmed, assured, and I needed to marshal all my resources to hear him out.

"I don't know how much time I have left, but I want it to be with you," he emphasized. "I don't want to share you."

Not much time left? I knew he had two life-threatening conditions, but I thought they were under control. Was he hiding something? What was he enjoining me to do?

My brother needed my help, but my vow was to my husband, for better or worse, and my brother had to leave. And no, he was not happy about it. I could see it in the way he walked, held his head, spoke with us at the table. But the last thing he wanted to do was jeopardize my marriage. That was something he couldn't live with.

My brother certainly recognized that his illness amid the pandemic had taken a toll on all three of us. After he returned home, I took care of his wound while Allen elder-proofed our home. He installed a bar assembly for the side of my brother's bed and grab bars in the bathrooms. At a nurse's recommendation, we secured our Turkish carpets and ordered a medical device for my brother to wear around his neck to alert emergency facilities if he fell. However, it often awakened us in the middle of the night when there was no emergency.

After several months at home, my brother's health had improved, and he was able to take walks, get together with friends, and drive again. He was perhaps 80 percent back to the condition he had been in before his surgery, but our marriage had not improved. Moreover, quite a bit of the dinner table conversation was between me and my brother, reminiscing about family and old times. Allen felt left out. There was more.

"You're easily distracted, absent-minded," Allen said. "You're worn out, emotionally and physically drained."

The changes brought on by the pandemic worsened the situation. When I off-the-cuff mentioned that I'd love to take off for a week on the Big Island,

Allen bristled.

"Even if we weren't in the midst of a pandemic and could go on vacation without him, your brother will be with us," he said. "We would have to arrange for his care, and then you would be constantly checking to see if he was okay."

Allen was right. Amid the strain, we had both become more remote. Allen retreated to his upstairs aerie to create inventions while I buried myself in a novel. I tried to write, but that was going poorly. A newspaper article that should have taken me four hours took an entire weekend of shuffling paragraphs around. Then after I sent it in and read the edited version, I caught a major mistake. My mistake. Was I disintegrating?

"I want my wife back," my husband repeated. "You need to check your priorities. When your parents were dying, and you had to take off for New York, I understood that. It was your duty. With your brother, I wasn't consulted. You put your commitment to him above everything else."

My vow on February 13, 2000, was to my husband. What were my responsibilities to him? With that in mind, I began inquiring about assisted living and other housing possibilities. One well-recommended facility was nearby and affordable, but we found the atmosphere depressing, institutional. The average age was eighty-seven. Other facilities were far beyond our budget. With the help of a friend, we found a family-run senior residence with a unit that overlooked a pool and redwoods that the owner had planted some forty-five years ago. It wasn't assisted living, but it provided meals, light housekeeping, and a range of activities. An acquaintance who lived there said she was quite contented.

The residence provided a congenial community for my brother, who made friends quickly. He came to realize that it was a wise, and an inevitable, decision. Meanwhile, with just the two of us at home, we could live more spontaneously. We could forage if we didn't feel like cooking or take off for a weekend without arranging my brother's care. We were no longer a threesome, but we were still a family.

PART V

TRAVELING ON

CHAPTER 49

SOON WE'LL HOP ON A PLANE–OR CALTRAIN*

Winter 2020–21

*P*aris to Zurich. New Orleans to St. Paul. Russia and the Baltic Sea. I pile the pamphlets on the coffee table. Then I toss out the guides that end with 2021 and leaf through the 2022–2023 trips. River voyages. Ocean expeditions. Amazon adventures. Undiscovered Adriatic. I think I'm ready for adventure. Is adventure ready for me? We are booked for a South American cruise set to leave in December 2021, but we wonder if it will ever leave port.

My husband shrugs and smiles, gauging my mood. Restlessness, optimism, or magical thinking? Maybe all three. It's been two years since I stepped onto an international flight and hugged my youngest granddaughter, who lives in East Yorkshire. My son and his family were supposed to visit us for Thanksgiving 2020. The best-laid plans.

---

* An earlier version of this chapter appeared February 19, 2021, in *J. The Jewish News of Northern California*.

Since Covid, I've hopped on Caltrain and BART only a few times to head to San Francisco, where I used to work and attend the theater and symphony. Now, getting on and off trains takes longer, and when I reach the platform, pedestrians rush past me. Escalators are awkward. Long staircases are problematic. And the elevators don't always work.

Not long ago, we were world travelers who traveled to five continents. In 2020, we barely left Palo Alto. On Hanukkah, we lit candles with extended family via Zoom and shared latkes with next-door neighbors. Instead of sitting around a Thanksgiving table with my daughter and her family, we packaged the meal that I cooked for them and then we ate by ourselves. On Christmas Day, we stayed home and Zoomed with family.

The pandemic was only part of the reason for our stay-at-home life. Our bodies are no longer ourselves. In 2000, when we married, we were middle-aged. Then we became the young-old. Now we don't know what rung we're on, and our balance is shaky.

Can we manage foreign railway stations? Escalators? Stairs? Cobblestones? It's not junior year abroad anymore, I say to myself, recalling my hitchhiking adventures in the 1960s. I'd like to think I can still rush around London, dragging a suitcase behind me as I hop on a double-decker bus. But these days, navigating Heathrow is a challenge.

We try to focus on what we can do, rather than what is no longer possible—but it's hard. We take walks, we cook together, and we sing our way through the day.

George Burns said that when he awoke, he'd check the obituaries. If he didn't see his name, he would eat breakfast. When I check the obits, if the decedent—in funeral home parlance—is eighty-eight, or ninety-eight, I figure I have another ten or twenty years. If the decedent is younger than I am, I figure I beat the grim reaper. For today.

After emailing his blood pressure and weight to Dr. David, my husband turns to me and says, "You know, staying alive is a full-time job."

I look at him, and as is our wont when things are in danger of getting macabre, I burst into song. "Ah, ha, ha, ha, stayin' alive, stayin' alive," I sing, strutting around the kitchen with one arm in the air.

He joins my geriatric disco swing, wiggling his arms in the air and laughing. Then we hug.

Soon, we may cruise again. Soon, we may hop on a plane. But tonight, we are here. So we dance.

CHAPTER 50

THIS WASN'T THE CRUISE WE SIGNED UP FOR[*]

December 2021–January 2022

Travel inevitably brings snafus: despite our well-thought-out packing lists, I could write a chapter on what we forgot to pack and what we should have left at home, like a beach coverup. Mostly, we shrug off such mishaps. But when the travel bug goes head-to-head with the coronavirus, anticipated adventures can quickly become misadventures. The saving grace is we have stories, and sometimes they hit print and go global. That's what happened with our long-awaited South American cruise.

"What, are you crazy?"

"Boy, are you brave!"

We are neither crazy nor brave—just itching to hit the high seas because we love sailing. After our congregation canceled our March 2020 trip to Greece

---

[*]   A version of this story ran January 13, 2022, in *J. The Jewish News of Northern California*.

and Israel, we languished landlocked for two years. Our last major trip was a November 2019 Portuguese Viking River cruise.

In March 2021, we thought Covid was ebbing. Aware that our use-by dates were narrowing as we aged, we signed up for a Viking Ocean cruise titled "South America & the Chilean Fjords." On this touted "journey to the end of the world," we hoped to hike in the Andes; strut among five species of penguins in the Falklands; and tour Ushuaia, Argentina, the southernmost city in the world. We planned to fill our buckets with wonderment at the Iguazu Falls.

Then along came Omicron, and our buckets slowly sprang leaks.

Even before December 19, when we left the Bay Area for Santiago, Chile, the Falklands canceled our visit because of Covid concerns. Then, our pre-trip jitters went into overdrive. The Chilean government required us to undergo a PCR test for Covid within seventy-two hours of our departure. We hoped we would receive the results before we boarded our flights, but we had no such assurance. Adding to the stress, my husband underwent an emergency tooth extraction two days before we left home. Then, as if our negative PCR tests and the proof of three vaccination doses were not enough, Chile demanded more documentation. A day or two before we left, Chile required us to fill out a cryptic C19 entry certificate showing proof of traveler's insurance and our "quarantine address."

When we arrived at the airport in Santiago, officials perused our paperwork and sent us to an airport lab for yet another Covid PCR test. Fortunately, we made the grade, but we never again saw the casual Southern Californians who stood in front of us in line at the airport and told us they had ignored emails from Viking. Presumably, they were among half-a-dozen potential cruisegoers sent back to the States for failure to fill out Chile's paperwork properly. After we arrived at our Santiago hotel, we were told not to leave our room until our test results came back negative. Then the next day, Viking cruises sent a crew to our hotel to administer another PCR test. The result is we spent the better part of two days marooned in the hotel and had only one short bus tour of Santiago. Meanwhile, Chile required us to file reports of our Covid status for ten days.

There's more: After we boarded the Viking *Jupiter* at Valparaiso, our state-room attendant smiled and handed us two test tubes for us to spit into so our saliva could be tested in the ship's onboard laboratory, a process we repeated each day. Our temperature was also checked daily, usually on our way into breakfast. Hand-sanitizing devices were mounted throughout the ship, and we were required to wear masks except while eating, drinking, or resting in our stateroom. We also wore tracking devices around our necks that would not only reveal our location on or off the ship but whether we had been in contact with someone who tested positive.

Early in the cruise, undersubscribed with only 314 passengers on a ship that holds 930, fourteen passengers were taken off the ship, including actor Liev Schreiber, who posted an Instagram video of himself dancing while quarantined in his Punta Arenas, Chile, hotel room.* However, Chile refused to let the rest of us disembark. Argentina followed suit when we docked at Ushuaia, where I sighed as I stood on deck, taking in the glaciers and mountain peaks. Argentina also canceled our stop at Puerto Madlyn, where we looked forward to a proper tea in a settlement founded by Welsh immigrants and a trek amid the penguins at Punta Tombo.

On December 30, 2021, the CDC advised Americans not to take cruises. That advice came a bit late for us, but to tell you the truth, our onboard cocoon was far safer than our homeport, where both our house sitter and my brother, each fully vaccinated, had contracted Covid. Our house sitter, who flew from New York to escape the cold, thought he may have contracted Covid in flight or in the airports.

During eight straight days at sea, we sailed past fjords and the breathtaking Amalia Glacier and rounded rocky Cape Horn, sailing from the Pacific to the Atlantic Ocean. We circled Hornos Island, but we neither hiked in the Andes nor spotted a penguin.

---

* Liev Schreiber (@lievschreiber), "Covid quarantine in Chile," Instagram post (December 28, 2021), https://www.instagram.com/p/CYCTN1NlsRI/

With Argentina out of the question, the captain sailed to the friendlier Uruguayan resort city of Punta del Este, which had not been on the schedule. When my husband got off the tour bus at a site commemorating the 1939 British victory of the HMS *Ajax* over the German ship *Graf Spee,* he lay down on the ground to embrace it.

On January 6, after a fun trip to Montevideo's Baar Fun Fun, where superb tango dancers pulled my husband onto the dance floor, I was sitting in the ship's theater for a port talk about the following day's excursions to Buenos Aires and our own flight to Iguazu Falls. I was more than primed for adventure.

Just as shore excursion manager Christopher McPherson was unveiling the possibilities for the following day—from visiting Evita Perón's final resting place to evening tango performances—the voice of Captain Erik Egede Saabye boomed over the loudspeaker. McPherson's face fell. No Buenos Aires, no Iguazu Falls, no Argentina. Period. McPherson had been looking forward to taking us to Iguazu himself.

The bottom line: we spent two extra days on board, docked in Montevideo, enjoying a splendid visit to a winery in the Uruguayan countryside, where we sampled a luscious port, among other wines. Meanwhile, Viking rearranged our transportation home and organized a charter to fly most of the passengers from Montevideo to Miami.

On January 10, we awakened at 3:00 a.m. for a bus ride to the small Montevideo airport, where our flight to Miami took off several hours later. When we arrived in Miami that evening, most of the passengers located their luggage. We did not. We scrambled, luggageless, to catch an 8:30 p.m. flight to San Francisco and missed it. A Viking representative personally shepherded us to the airport Sheraton, where he delivered our luggage after midnight. We awakened at 5:30 a.m. on January 11, bolted down a quick breakfast, and caught an 8:30 a.m. flight to SFO. As a result, we probably clocked six hours of sleep in two nights.

Friends asked us about our adventure, but other than the final trip home, we enjoyed nearly three weeks of peace, quiet, and fabulous meals. With more than four hundred crew members to wait on three hundred passengers, the experience became sybaritic. We never made it to the gym, but we took advantage of the extra sea days to book two massages each.

"Even though we were ship-bound for eight days, I welcomed the time to unwind," my husband said.

Arlene Verona of Florida said she "gained a serenity" over our time at sea, adding that a fellow passenger noticed that cruise-goers seemed to have "lost the bags under their eyes." So did I.

With topflight entertainment, informative lectures, filet mignon topped with foie gras, blinis with caviar, and orgiastic pastries, what could have been a nightmare quickly turned into a dreamy vacation—one in which I learned to roll with the tide. One of the highlights was afternoon tea in the ship's Wintergarden, where classical duo Ildi, a cellist from Hungary, and her husband, pianist Adrian from Spain, played soothing music. In the ship's theater, Ukraine-born Canadian musician Dennis Daye—who could play piano with his left hand and trumpet with his right, or double up on accordion and ocarina—added a couple of additional performances. He played four-hand piano with the onboard pianist Sasha, and he also accompanied the ship's singers, arranging the music himself.

With three short self-led Shabbat services every Friday night, we met other Jewish passengers and shared our traditions, which varied immensely. One woman from Texas asked whether our Los Altos Hills congregation was one of those synagogues with a female rabbi and a guitar-playing cantor. We smiled, said yes to both, and changed the subject.

Most of the passengers were frequent cruisers whose previous trips had been canceled by Covid, and many were already planning their next trips. As for us, we were happy to be home—for a while.

CHAPTER 51

*COVID CROSSES US IN CORNWALL** *

June–July 2022

Squished in a window seat on our return flight from Heathrow to San Francisco, I had ten hours to reflect on my star-crossed journey, our second international trip in 2022. After a bout with Covid, I was returning home with muscle cramps and congestion. The next day my husband—the only one in our Cornwall cottage who didn't contract Covid—awoke at home with a feverish flu. Go figure.

I should have anticipated the tenor of this trip when we first arrived in London on June 28. Allen couldn't find his wallet, which contained his credit cards, cash, and driver's license. The wallet never made it to London. Instead, it was waiting safely in an obscure San Francisco Airport security office. Despite our TSA PreCheck Global Entry status, my husband was asked to empty his

---

* An earlier version of this chapter appeared August 11, 2022, in *J. The Jewish News of Northern California*

pockets, remove his belt, and then take out his passport. He reclaimed his pass-port and belt but forgot about the wallet in a separate tray. Thank God I had credit cards, and we weren't renting a car.

Over the course of our marriage, adventure and misadventure have had a way of finding us, whether it's a purse-snatcher in Barcelona or an angry Roo-sevelt elk in the redwoods. But our week in Cornwall wasn't meant to be an adventure. Instead, I was looking forward to visiting gardens, galleries, and rugged coasts, and wallowing in clotted Cornish cream.

My son and his family, who live in Yorkshire, had rented a three-bedroom cottage in Cornwall, where we would spend a week together. Not having seen my granddaughter since 2019, we were overjoyed when she and her parents met our train in Truro on a Friday afternoon.

But our joy was short-lived. On Sunday morning, I awoke with a fever, tested positive for Covid, and spent five days quarantined in an upstairs bedroom, looking out the window at a lone gravestone of a woman named Catherine. My son and Allen carried my meals up the stairs on a tray and communi-cated through Facebook Messenger. Banished from the bedroom, Allen slept on pillows on the living room floor, Meanwhile, I napped, checked the news on my iPad, did crossword puzzles, and finished *Sarum*, Edward Rutherfurd's 1,039-page novel about Salisbury's history.

Fortunately, I was never terribly ill, and toward the end of that week I took walks around town with my husband. Fully vaccinated and double boosted, my case of Covid was the equivalent of a twenty-four-hour virus. Had I been forearmed, I could have traveled with a just-in-case prescription for Paxlovid, which other US travelers carried abroad. Unfortunately, I was unable to obtain the prescription in the UK, as I wasn't an emergency case. On the one hand, I didn't contend with post-Paxlovid rebound, one of the side effects of the drug. However, after ruining everybody's holiday, I *was* plagued by post-Covid guilt. Why hadn't I self-tested before I arrived in Cornwall? Where did I become infected? Over tea in Kensington Palace, at the Victoria and Albert Museum, in the Roman baths at Bath?

Our Cornwall rental ended the following Friday, and just as we were about to leave for the train station, my son texted us. He and his wife had contracted Covid. They couldn't fly home to Yorkshire as planned, and the airline wouldn't credit them for a future flight.

We offered to be caregivers and spend time with our granddaughter, but I had already caused enough chaos. Unfortunately, several days later, my granddaughter came down with Covid, delaying their return home by eight days. We could help financially — the delay had cost them more than $2,000—but we could do nothing to ameliorate a holiday gone awry.

My husband and I grabbed our suitcases and ambled down the hill to the railroad station a mile or so away. Still concerned about contagion, we canceled plans to dine in Bath with University of Glasgow housemate and famed astrophysicist Jocelyn Bell Burnell. Ironically, she emailed back that she, too, tested positive for Covid, so it wasn't meant to be.

We made the best of our remaining time in the UK. On our return to Bath from Cornwall, we immersed ourselves in Jane Austen, Roman remnants, and Georgian architecture, and relished a gooey-rich afternoon tea at our hotel. Moving on to Salisbury, we arrived at the railway station only to discover no cabs were available. Once again, we schlepped our suitcases a mile to our hotel, a sixteenth-century inn where I had the best Sunday roast in my memory. The next day, we explored ancient Sarum, the hilltop site of ancient ruins described in Rutherfurd's book, and the magnificent cathedral, which displays the original Magna Carta in its chapter house.

Upon returning to London, we met up with my stepdaughter and her family, who were also visiting, and took our grandsons to the Churchill War Rooms, exploring the underground bunker where the prime minister and his officials had holed up during the Blitz.

At the end of a long flight home, I was glad to escape Britain's blistering summer heat wave. Cornwall's gardens will await another visit, but I looked forward to tooling around my own garden.

Meanwhile, I obtained another inoculation, this time the bivalent COVID-19 booster. But there is no vaccine for the travel bug, and after barely seeing my granddaughter during a weeklong trip, the skies are calling. With luck, I won't be squished in flight, and Allen will arrive with his wallet and credit cards.

CHAPTER 52

'GRATEFUL FOR THE MEMORIES'*

October 2022

When I applied for my Real ID driver's license in 2022, I listed my hair color as gray and my height as five feet. I have lost an inch, my hair is no longer brown, and when I look in the mirror, my mother looks back at me. The full-length mirror is scarier. Whose body is this anyway?

I first noticed age creeping up on me after my second child was born, when fastening my skirts required a safety pin instead of a button. When I bemoaned my changing body to my doctor, he said, "Janet, you can't get from age twenty to age forty without aging."

Eighty is not the new forty, fifty, or sixty, and the signs of aging are more pronounced. I can laugh at the spoof of "My Favorite Things": "Cadillacs and cataracts and hearing aids and glasses." I drive a Prius, not a Cadillac, which

---

* An earlier version of this chapter appeared October 28, 2022, in *J. The Jewish News of Northern California.*

was the car of my parents' generation, but I do wear hearing aids, when I remember to put them in, and I also wear glasses. At night, I see auras around streetlights, which at first fascinated me, wondering why my husband didn't see them. When I told my ophthalmologist, she shook her head. "We're watching those cataracts," she said. Another C-word.

So far, I have been spared the Big C, and I still have all my body parts, including my wisdom teeth. However, my daughter, at midlife, recently underwent a double mastectomy and a hysterectomy. Neither of us has the BRCA gene. Why did breast cancer strike her? Yet my daughter feels fortunate. She sees an expected survival rate of at least five years as a blessing. Should I feel blessed as well? My father lived until almost eighty-five, my mother until almost eighty-seven. If I have another five years, I have two partly written novels that I need to finish. I'd better get busy.

I believe it's our works, and our words, that outlive us. The stories and the memories we leave behind. When I'm asked about the afterlife, I have been known to say glibly, "It's none of my business. I don't know and I don't care." Yet I recognize that thoughts of a better place beyond this world bring comfort to folks during times of pain and loss. I'm glad they have that solace, but I believe my only business is here. Will I get it done in time? There's always a deadline.

In truth, freelancing as a writer and editor has kept me going, even when I couldn't go anywhere. When the pandemic first struck and I was confined with misdiagnosed Covid, editing a travel book lifted my spirits.

During tough times, we try to do what brings us joy. For me, it's baking buttermilk scones; cooking for friends and family; gardening; listening to ABBA, Cass Elliot, and Simon and Garfunkel, the duo whom I first encountered at Forest Hills High School when they were Tom and Jerry. Harmonizing with my husband is another upper. For me, music is a hotline to the sublime, particularly during the Jewish High Holidays. But if I would rather wallow, Spotify has a self-pity list that includes "Everything Happens to Me," "I Guess That's Why They Call It the Blues," and "It's My Party."

My husband, eighty-five at this writing, has made his own adjustments to aging. He still sings solos, consults, invents, and applies for new patents—but he also takes more naps. There are things he can't do, and things he shouldn't do. He knows wielding a hammer will result in hours of pain, so he may call upon his grandson to complete the task. He recently relocated his office from the loft to a front bedroom because taking the stairs repeatedly caused problems with his knees, not to mention his bladder. We both wear Depends while flying, just in case. But we still plan to travel, just not as frequently as we did ten years ago. As I often say, it's not junior year abroad anymore. When younger travelers offer to help with our luggage as we get off trains, we gratefully accept their offers. Why deny them the opportunity to do a mitzvah?

In my forties, when I was working for the *Oakland Tribune*, I interviewed a therapist and author on her experience of aging. "At eighty," she told me, "you do less."

"You do it more slowly," said Barbara August, a retired therapist in my Zumba Gold class at the Palo Alto Jewish Community Center, where we both enjoy dance movement at a comfortable pace.

"Every day is a milestone," Alayne Greenwald said in a life-review video on the Stanford Medicine website.[*] When she turned eighty and was studying Farsi, she joined a Stanford group and spent six weeks in Iran on her own, writing a book about the experience. At age ninety-two, she and her husband, Alan, who was turning ninety-seven, were blessed at their synagogue on their seventy-third anniversary. Why seventy-three? Why not?

Over their years together, she and Alan, who live in the Vi, a senior community in Palo Alto, traveled to seven continents and lived in Italy and Israel. Now Alan's heart condition precludes travel.

"I'm grateful for the memories," Alayne said, adding that gratitude is "one of the things that comes with age. I'm grateful that I'm walking and talking," she added, noting that she swims seven days a week and walks two miles.

---

[*] "Patient Videos," *Stanford Medicine*, med.stanford.edu/letter/videos.html

Gratitude is one of the soul traits earmarked in *The Spiritual Practice of Good Actions* by Greg Marcus, my teacher of American Mussar and a rabbinical student. "Mussar teaches that the gratitude soul trait governs our ability to recognize the good in any situation," he writes.

I try to keep that in mind as I step out my door to grab a handful of cherry tomatoes and parsley, grateful that the squirrels, which have ravished the Early Girl tomatoes, seem to ignore the tiny Sun Golds.

At eighty, I'm also grateful that I became part of a Jewish community after a long slumber. I am grateful for friends and family, which include four children and eight grandchildren. I am grateful for god Google, which finds me the name, word, or concept that often eludes my brain. And I'm especially grateful to the *Jewish Bulletin*, forerunner of *J. The Jewish News of Northern California*, which hired me as a copy editor during a low period in 1993, and where I found the love of my life six years later through a silly singles ad.

CHAPTER 53

NEW YEAR'S EVE IN A DOWNPOUR

What good is sitting alone in your room?
"CABARET," FROM *CABARET*

December 31, 2022

Determined to not let the Bay Area's reported "second wettest day on record"* dampen our holiday spirit, we stuffed our backpacks with festive apparel, parked the Prius at BART, and headed to San Francisco to ring in 2023.

Amid new threats of Covid, we weren't about to revive our New Year's Eve sing-alongs and host a spreader event. Instead, we orchestrated a party of two, a romantic overnight escapade to San Francisco. Why let a deluge wash out our plans?

---

* Drew Tuma, Spencer Christian, and Justin Mendoza, "New Year's Eve storm 2nd wettest day on record for San Francisco," *ABC7 News* (January 1, 2023), abc7news.com/san-francisco-wettest-day-record-bay-area-storm-atmospheric-river/12638575/

Friends thought we were crazy, adventurous, reckless—or all three. Had my mother been alive, she would have tried to dissuade us. Now our offspring have taken up the mantle of caution. While we were hydroplaning near the BART station, we received a text from Allen's younger daughter: "Are you still going?"

"Yes. Allen says to tell you he walked in the Baylands this morning, with lightning rods," I texted.

Later, as we descended the escalator to the BART platform, Allen's daughter reached him on his cell phone. She suggested that we drive straight to the city and avoid walking in the rain. Too late. But it wasn't too late for our tryst, even in our eighties.

We sloshed through downtown streets, checked into the Nikko hotel, took a short nap, and relished a five-course Japanese-inspired meal. After dinner, we headed downstairs to Feinstein's, where we donned party hats, sipped champagne, and welcomed the new year with panache. Michael Feinstein (a partner in the hotel's nightclub) wasn't playing. Instead, the stars of the night were Jarrod Spector and Kelli Barrett, accompanied by a stellar band. Spector, who played Frankie Valli in *Jersey Boys* on Broadway, wooed the audience with "Can't Take My Eyes Off You," and Allen wooed me, singing softly so only I could hear him. Meanwhile, Barrett did an amazing Liza Minnelli–style "Cabaret," among other numbers, and I could not keep from singing.

Fortunately, by New Year's Day the rain had abated. We toted our backpacks to a Japanese restaurant for a ramen breakfast and then headed to Union Square, where we watched the ice skaters. Although I was tempted, hitting the ice was one risk we didn't take. The only time Allen and I went ice skating together, he hit the ice and wound up in the ER with a concussion. Winter Lodge compensated us with free passes that we passed on to a friend.

We continued down Stockton Street, reminiscing as we passed the building that formerly housed FAO Schwarz. That's where we'd met in 1999, playing together with our feet atop the mat piano immortalized in *Big*. That keyboard is gone, but we're still playing, still making music.

High on our memories, we stopped for a cappuccino on Market Street. Since San Francisco's Museum of Modern Art was open, we spent a delightful afternoon amid the surprising work of Joan Brown (1938–1990).

This California artist took chances and kept reinventing herself, moving from the nondescript abstracts of her student days to the whimsical cat paintings and more spiritually inspired works of her later years. Brown married four times, became an accomplished ballroom dancer and swimmer, and nearly drowned in icy waters while swimming from Alcatraz to Aquatic Park. Brown died tragically in India when a concrete turret collapsed at the Eternal Heritage Museum, killing her instantly and destroying the obelisk she was mounting. She was only fifty-two. But what a legacy she left behind.

An artist takes chances and evolves. So do writers and engineer-inventors. Allen and I continue to veer off course, exploring new paths, reinventing ourselves. Our time is not open-ended. We set priorities. However, priorities, like sands, inevitably shift. We wind up in a place we had never planned to visit, even as we age in place, because nothing really stays in place. "The only emperor is the emperor of ice-cream."[*]

---

[*]   Wallace Stevens, "The Emperor of Ice-Cream."

ACKNOWLEDGMENTS

Thank you to Mascot Books, imprint of Amplify Publishing, for taking a chance on me; to acquisitions director Jess Cohn and production editor Rachel Applebach, who guided me; and to designer Shannon Sullivan, who created an amazing cover.

To my fabulous web designer, Roberta Morris (leaveittoberta.com), and photographer Suz McFadden (SuzMcFaddenphoto.com), who made me look good.

To author Esther Erman, who copyedited and provided publishing advice; to Barbara Leeds, who has an uncanny eye for typos; and to news historian and retired *Oakland Tribune* managing editor Eric Newton, who pointed me to publishers when agents were ghosting me.

To Sylvia Halloran and fellow students in her writing classes at Mountain View-Los Altos Adult Education, who read my work chapter by chapter.

To my Tuesday writers' group: Kathleen Canrinus and Denise Kiser, who critiqued an early draft; David Vaughan, who dreamed up the incredible title; and James Sweeney and Bill Janssen, who offered invaluable advice.

To Joyce Maynard, whose all-day memoir workshop helped me refocus my story, and author Myra Strober, who read a late draft and erased my doubts.

To the staff at *J. The Jewish News of Northern California*: editor emerita Sue Fishkoff, who invited me to write a column for seniors; editors Sue Barnett, Andy Altman-Orr, Andrew Esensten, Natalie Weinstein, and David A.M. Wilensky, who shepherded my copy; and retired editors Marc Klein and Woody Weingarten, who gave me a second chance in journalism.

To the late Roy Aarons, my mentor at the *Oakland Tribune*.

To the Aurora Singers and HaShirim, who keep me in tune; to spiritual director Peg Krome; to Rabbi Allen Bennett, who presided over my bat mitzvah and wedding; and to friends and clergy at Congregation Beth Am. Special thanks to American Mussar maven Greg Marcus, who taught me something about patience, gratitude, and equanimity.

I am eternally grateful for the support of my husband, Allen Podell; my brother, Robert E. Silver; and my children, Nicole Ghent Wickenhiser, Randall Ghent, and Shani and Phoenix Podell.

Finally, to my parents, Robert Martin Silver and Carolyn Hirsch Silver, who filled the house with books and encouraged me to be a journalist.

J. The Jewish News of Northern California and the Bay Area News Group, publisher of the former *Oakland Tribune*, granted permission to reprint material from my columns.

ABOUT THE AUTHOR

*J*anet Silver Ghent, the daughter of a New York publishing executive, grew up in a house full of books and was determined to write them. With two degrees in English—a bachelor's cum laude from Oberlin and a master's from the University of Michigan, plus study at University of Glasgow—she considered herself doubly unemployable. Nonetheless, she became an award-winning journalist, writing features for San Francisco Bay Area newspapers. Now semiretired, she is a columnist for *J. The Jewish News of Northern California*, where she was senior editor. Janet lives in Silicon Valley with her husband, an engineer-inventor-baritone. They sing together in three chorales and travel worldwide. At home, they enjoy time with their four children and eight grandchildren. A self-described haphazard gourmet, Janet grows her own herbs and takes pride in her pesto.